Rev. Carlton Brown has captured the e̶   ninety year history and vision in this book. There are few leaders or churches that have the extraordinary blending of global and community mission. It is an important book for students of progressive urban church models.

Dr. Mac Pier
President
Concerts of Prayer Greater New York
The New York City Leadership Center

Bethel Gospel Assembly is one of the premier churches in New York City because of its emphasis on holistic ministry, unwavering faith in the Bible as the Word of God and casting local and international missions work in obedience to the Great Commission. If there is anyone capable of teaching how a church can successfully transition an unbeliever to a committed disciple of Christ, it is my dear friend Bishop Carlton T. Brown.

Bishop Joseph G. Mattera
Presiding Bishop of Christ Covenant Coalition
Overseeing Bishop of Resurrection Church
Sunset Park, NY

'Til Death Do We S.H.O.P.

Taking Hold of a Ministry Approach
that is Making a Difference in a
Spiritually Indifferent World.

✠

By Carlton T. Brown

All text written by Carlton T. Brown.
Carlton T. Brown Ministries, Inc.
244 Fifth Avenue, Suite 2898, New York, NY 10001
Phone: 212/591-1500, Website: www.ctbrown.org
Email: questions and comments to info@ctbrown.org
or ministry requests to booking@ctbrown.org
First published in 2009, by Welstar Publications, Inc.
628 Lexington Avenue, Brooklyn, NY 11221
Phone: 718/453-6557, Fax: 718/338-1454
E-mail: drbatson@optonline.net
or editor@welstarpublications.com
ISBN: 978-0-938503-36-1
10 9 8 7 6 5 4 3 2 1

Editing/Book Design/Typography
by Kate Stephenson.
Text set in Garamond and BaskervilleOld Face.

Cover Design by Clive Williamson,
Ontarget Communications

Carlton Brown Photos courtesy of Shahar Azran Photography, LLC.

Seekers of the blessed
Hope,
Ordained for divine
Purpose!

FOREWORD

We live in an era of vivid change. Old standards and conventions that prevailed even forty years ago have fallen away in the world and the church. With the waning of the Civil Rights movement and Vietnam War dissent, change gradually but stubbornly emerged. By the late 1970s, our society had begun to morph into the secularized, hyper-materialistic, post-Christian and post-modern society that has become fully manifested in the early 21st Century. At the same time, we witnessed bitterly disappointing setbacks in civil rights and the deadly infusion of drugs into our urban communities.

Along with these morally degrading forces, the leaven of secular liberalism has endowed starkly immoral movements with counterfeit civil rights agendas and alleged moral imperatives. The serpent-like rationale of this age is seductive: women's rights are ultimately defined by the moral "choice" regarding unborn human life; people caught in the grip of homo-erotic desire are declared a "community" with "rights" and "identity" issues comparable to struggling African Americans and Latinos. The faithful church has witnessed this cultural insanity with a kind of incredulous dismay. One is reminded of the tragic observation of ancient Euripides, who concluded that those "whom the gods would destroy they first make mad."

Of course, this tragedy has not taken place in a cultural vacuum. Along with the rotting influence of post-Christian secularism, our society has increasingly succumbed to a stupefying appetite for amusement (literally "a-musement" means "non-musement", or "non-thinking") and an overriding prejudice toward informality. While neither is bad in itself, as *cultural standards of being*, amusement and informality are destructive, diminishing forces. People who prefer amusement to critical thinking are easily fooled, invariably misled and often corrupted. People who live by the rule of informality generally become people without commitments, without discipline and without godliness. Witness a nation where television "news" programs disproportionately feature sports and celebrity coverage to the exclusion of current events worldwide; where young people in college are ignorant of basic political and geographical facts; where adults are tattooing and piercing their bodies as a matter of fashion; and where modesty's ongoing retreat has left women's clothing styles showing more flesh and form than ever before.

As far as the faithful church is concerned, it appears that we have already lost the "culture wars" of North America. We are privately outraged by the advances of both secular liberals and greed-and-warmongering conservatives. Thoughtful, godly and justice-oriented Christians are caught between the proverbial "rock and a hard place" in every election year, knowing that a vote for either party is a kind of dance with the devil. Consoling ourselves with the idea of voting for the lesser of two evils is getting tired and is wearing thin.

Rather than playing the role of a "city on a hill", Christians are rapidly becoming a community marginalized and excluded by the reigning doctrine of church-state separation. Although church-state separation was originally intended to protect the religious community from the intrusion of government, secularists in our age have turned the tables with a vengeance. The religious community is not supposed to speak or participate in the political arena of the nation.

Even at a popular level, ask yourself when was the last time that you saw a clergyman invited to speak on a television talk show? There was a time when religious leaders were actually taken seriously as social and cultural experts; but in the post-Christian age of Oprah and Dr. Phil, the insight and opinion of the church has been pushed aside. Today's moral experts are psychologists and celebrities (and in television, the two roles are increasingly blurred).

Meanwhile the emasculated minister's role is to "marry and bury". The recent uproar over the Reverend Jeremiah Wright's jeremiad (the use of the term here is more than clever) against "America" was not just based about offending the racial narcissism and "patriotic" idolatry of the USA.

Many were also offended because Wright displayed the audacity of a clergyman who presumed to exercise the prophetic role of his ministry within the community. Ministers are to be seen and not heard. If they are heard, they are to be heard only comforting, assuaging and encouraging the status quo–minded listener.

Things have changed inside the church, too. For those of us who grew up in the "old school" gospel-preaching, we are often reminded of the paradigm shift that has taken place among so-called evangelicals and gospel-preaching Christians. To paraphrase an old Chevrolet ad, the contemporary Christian church truly is not our parent's church. Indeed, as some so-called post-modern Christians believe, this change is all well and good—old wine-skins cannot hold new wine, they say, and we are living at a time when the church must be redefined.

Not long ago I was in attendance at a church planning seminar, during which I overheard a zealous urban missionary (freshly arrived in New York City from the suburbs) unfold his strategy for starting a church in the Big Apple. "People don't want sermons anymore. The age of the sermon is over," he confidently declared. "What people want is feedback!" I suspect that he has since learned some lessons that have taken him back to the drawing board. However, at least his presumption serves to remind us that all of the winds of change that are blowing through the church today are not good currents of the Holy Spirit.

Dare we admit that ill winds are puffing the sails of many popular religious and para-church movements today? Are we prepared to admit that perhaps we have thrown out the baby of orthodoxy with the bath water of an older generation? Do organizational dynamics and corporate leadership models *really* represent progress for the gospel and the church?

The challenge for the 21st Century pastor and Christian leadership in general is to discern and evaluate the winds of change, the movements and shifts in the course of ministry, and the presence of dangerous reefs upon which our churches could run aground. We live in an era when leadership seminars have taken precedence over doctrinal and exegetical interests, and when pastors in the local church are constantly standing in the shadows of highly successful and influential mega-church ministries that tend to provide the new paradigm of "successful" ministry in the 21st Century. In many cases, Christians have not only lost a sense of their own local church history, but of the larger history of Christian faith and doctrine.

What kind of Christianity is being broadcast worldwide when its major advocates are men and women who preach man-centered messages and present themselves as models of materialistic success and proponents of "prosperity"? Perhaps it is time to stop criticizing the Roman Church for banking the wealth of nations and sequestering the art of the Renaissance in the Vatican's treasury. At least that church's clergy are accountable to a single leader! The post-Protestant "evangelical" world is rife with televangelistic fiefdoms—little kingdoms run by non-denominational kings and queens who profit from the masses with no accountability to any denomination or biblically-based authority. As virtual gods-unto-themselves, they reign over the airwaves and disseminate whatever doctrine is expedient to their ongoing influence.

Insofar as race relations and the urban church are concerned, it is a foregone conclusion among most black and Latino Christians that the self-proclaimed evangelical "racial reconciliation" movement of the 1990s has died a hard death, largely due to the lack of courage in white evangelicals to focus upon urban ministry. Perhaps without realizing it, many of these aggressive urban missionaries are imitating their white liberal predecessors in the Civil Rights era as they pour into cities of our nation with sincere but messianic intent. While many have done some good, and some have done a great deal of good, there is often manifested a certain arrogance and presumption that was also known among their secular predecessors in the Civil Rights era. Though planting churches and forming para-church organizations in the name of "the city", many have done so without addressing the racism and racial narcissism of their own communities—that is, without actually laying a prophetic ax to the root of urban realities. Indeed, having established churches and para-church organizations, these same white leaders are quick to place themselves in the position of speaking for "the city". In doing so, they cannot help but manifest a cultural predisposition to *lead* Christians of color and *define* the agenda of urban ministry as well.

We should recall that the gadflies of white liberal narcissism in the Civil Rights era were the "angry" political philosophers among peoples of color that called for self-determination and a break with white activists. For instance, "Black Power" worried and even scared white liberals, even though it was mainly a call for black leadership and black political self-definition to prevail in the Civil Rights movement. To be sure, a similar reaction to white urban *missionary-ism* already exists in the private conversations of urban black and Latino missionaries. However, it goes without question that the most thoughtful leaders of the urban church are sensitive to the necessity of defining their ministries apart from white evangelical prerequisites.

In light of all this one may then ask, *Whither the urban church?* God being sovereign, we cannot presume to answer that question definitively. However, if our study of contemporary globalization and diversity tell us anything, it is that *as the urban church goes, so goes the church.*

Posed with such a question in the context that I have described, it has been an occasion of refreshing contemplation for me to read this thoughtful work by Bishop Carlton Brown. First, I have known the author for two decades and have witnessed his steady rise in ministry as a colleague and brother in Christ. When I met him in the late 1980s, he was an active committed and greatly loved youth pastor and elder in Bethel Gospel Assembly under the prestigious leadership of Bishop Ezra Williams. Like his predecessor, Bishop Brown knows the church "warp and woof".

A son of the church, he has labored in the urban context of Harlem and beyond, traveling nationally and internationally in mission efforts, and proving himself a superlative scholar in the context of seminary study. Since he assumed the pastorate of Bethel Gospel Assembly in 2000, he has faithfully followed the Lord's profile of "the head of the household", bringing forth from his treasure "things new and old" (Mat. 12:52). Apart from the faithful preaching of the prophetic and apostolic word, Bishop Brown has likewise shown an appreciation for and a dependence upon the traditions and convictions of Bethel's historic ministry while also bringing a new perspective to bear upon the church's role in the 21st Century. These aspects flow above and below the terrain of this work, so the reader may be assured that even as "wisdom is vindicated by her children" (Luke 7:35), the thesis of the book is proven by the integrity of his ministry and the undoubted testimony of Bethel Gospel Assembly's leadership in urban ministry for decades.

Til Death Do We S.H.O.P. is a catchy title, but this is more than a clever pastoral theology. As a multi-faceted and multi-layered reflection on ministry, mission and the roots of Bethel Gospel Assembly in Harlem, Bishop Brown as author is likewise the good steward of things new and old. He is well aware of the contemporary church and the issues highlighted above, just as he is clearly compelled by the "nagging question" that he says "should attach itself to every ministry", namely, "how does the manner in which we do church reflect God's purpose for the people we have been called to serve?" As a self-proclaimed "rational radical", the writer is calling for a great deal more from his readers than for them to embrace a set of programmatic goals and a vision statement in keeping with the contemporary bent toward reproducing organizational dynamics in the church. To the contrary, he challenges his readers to submit to the dynamic of Christ-centered transformation with the intention of "inspiring a movement in the body of Christ to transform whole communities for His glory."

This is a book about ministry—about the heart and soul of ministry, about servant and servant convictions, about the roots and fruits of the church, particularly one of the most successful and faithful gospel-preaching churches in the great urban village of Harlem, New York City. His work is thus premised upon the *process of ministry* through the *progress of the gospel.*

Sensitive to the necessity of moving with the Spirit of God, nevertheless the author is not afraid to criticize trends, for instance, what he calls "a misguided quest among many pastors to lead mega-churches" instead of aspiring "to the far more satisfying and loftier goal of embracing the *Mega God*." The truly successful church is the church that makes disciples according to a biblical model, even as it challenges the status quo within religious culture and in the world at large. Strategically, Bishop Brown argues, God's people must pursue biblically-based means toward establishing both "intrusive and practical" solutions to the challenges of ministry today.

Like any effective ministry instruction, this work contains what I would call practical parables. Parables, one may recall, are *illustrations placed next to principles* in order to cast greater light upon the truth set forth. Bishop Brown thus draws upon Scripture, upon his own experiences in ministry, and upon the dramatic history of Bethel Gospel Assembly in the most dynamic black community in the western world. Thus he skillfully blends the treasure of the past with the currents of contemporary ministry, all the while sustaining a strong commitment to Scripture and the requirements of God's kingdom. Notwithstanding his primary commitment to urban ministry, Bishop Brown thus presents the reader with workable structures and concepts for ministry that apply anywhere in the work of the Lord. His goal is undoubted: to train and encourage credible witnesses of the gospel that will engender "deliverance and final victory" for God's people.

The way before us is challenging. To borrow from a classical work, we live in both "the best of times and the worst of times." We seem to have an abundance of celebrity preachers and a dearth of prophets. We have many, many churches and many, many para-church ministries, yet the impact of the church seems uneven and perhaps inadequate to the times. However, God is still on the throne, the door for ministry is opened wide, and there are faithful ministries working effectively to advance the gospel in the world. Indeed with the effective strategy for ministry as set forth in this book, churches and individual believers cannot be counted out. Working in and through the "shopping" Christian church, the Holy Spirit may yet stir the chords of reform and revival in our nation and our world. After all, there are no sleeping giants in God's kingdom, only a sovereign King who moves in times and seasons as He sees fit.

These times and seasons are not for us to second-guess. We are not called to gaze upward but rather move forward. It is God's work to preserve and prove His own kingdom. It is our job to proclaim that kingdom by making disciples and faithfully witnessing to a fallen world concerning the sure and righteous judgment of the Lord. For this reason, our esteemed author shows us that shopping is serious kingdom business. *Seekers of the blessed Hope, Ordained for divine Purpose* is what shopping is all about. Ministry is about loving, learning and launching, says Bishop Carlton Brown—clearly reiterating the kingdom principles of Scripture. As we see from this work, shoppers are not engaged in a self-indulgent, self-serving endeavor, but are set upon the work of Christ, to "seek and save that which is lost." May you, the reader, enjoy and reflect upon this work, and then embark upon the great shopping quest for God's glory!

Louis A. DeCaro, Jr., Ph.D.
Alliance Theological Seminary, NYC

CONTENTS

ACKNOWLEDGEMENTS

This is just my humble deposit into the massive collection of papyruses in that grand library owned by time. However insignificant it may be, there are many people that contributed to the mind-set that makes this book a reality. It can be a very dangerous thing to make lists. I was going to do so, but I changed my mind. Since the original has been destroyed, only I know if your name appeared. Actually, it probably did, but as I began to think of all the names I needed to add, I surrendered that plan. So here is a very short list consisting of primarily family. The rest of you know who you are, and I am so grateful to you all. I will be taking the time to tell each of you individually just how much you meant to this project.

I thank my parents, Theophilus and Lois Priscilla Brown for teaching me about the love of God and stoking the love of learning and the power of ideas. Their faithfulness to God was realized in a home that produced a quiver full of saved, Holy Ghost–filled siblings for me to enjoy. Diane Joy (Ryan), Kevin and Yvette (Barclay, Esquire), thank you for being part of my foundation. Mom and Dad, I also want to thank you for taking all of us to Sunday School. I still have recollections of my teacher, the late Mrs. Margaret Chambers, reading us lessons from the little picture cards which cultivated for me this great enjoyment I continue to find in the world of books, and in time, resulted in my dabbling in writing poems, articles and the occasional short story.

To aunts, uncles, cousins, nephews and nieces and especially to my brothers and sister Thomas, Earl and Joan—what a wonderful family you are. I also must thank God for some special extended family members. I do thank God for the sound, passionate and humble leadership of Senior Pastor, Bishop Ezra N. Williams, whose considerable gift as a communicator of the Word of God captured my heart and imagination. Also for his spending hours "salting me down" in preparation for a ministry neither of us planned on. He is a true shepherd of the flock and will always be loved and respected.

Very special acknowledgement to my spiritual mother Dr. Ruth Onukwue, MD, whose commitment to young people and their potential paved the way for my involvement in missions, both in the city of New York and around the world. She was my leader and teacher, and today she serves under my leadership as our Missionary and Field Director of our ministries in South Africa. Thank you for your role as a healer of people, spiritually as well as physically.

To my dear friend Dr. Edgard Lashley, former President of the United Pentecostal Council of the Assemblies of God, a truly great leader and man of vision: I must say thank you for investing in my life by giving me the opportunity to serve in the position of National Missions Director of UPCAG, when so many others could not understand your selection. I will always treasure the many hours spent unpacking principles of ministry as well as our travel bags. Though now semi-retired in Barbados, your friendship and counsel is just as cherished today as it was fifteen years ago.

To "Big Man" Pastor Gordon Williams and "little Big Man" Minister Vincent Williams, my brothers through Spirit and experiences. We have gone a long way around the world together. Thanks for wonderful times and your support.

My Pastoral Assistant and sister in the Lord, Joyce Ford-Eady— thank you for your incredible creativity, support and faithfulness to the work of God.

To my Project Manager and spiritual daughter Ruth-Ann Wynter— you got it done. You are simply amazing.

To my anonymous friend, brother and teacher...thank you. You know what you did.

To my wonderful and very interesting children, Justin and Carla: thank you for always loving me and making it easy over the years of much traveling and late night emergency runs. I am proud of you and hope this book will not be an embarrassment to you (smile).

Most of all, to my beautiful and brilliant wife Lorna, who took over my heart when we came together at the altar over thirty-three years ago: You are the very special and very public source of my joy. You have put up with my insanity, trying to do so much more for me than God could have possibly asked and chiding me when not doing what God said to do. You have been after me to put my ideas in books since we came together thirty-five years ago. Every time you said "*I give up...*" you would still come back and say—"*When are you going to start writing?*" You have been with me through the bad and worse days, and have a way of making them feel like the best days. If no one else reads this book, I know you will be the one that will have committed it to memory. I love you and thanks for the push.

PROLOGUE

I learned a long time ago not to think of church as an organization but as an organism, but I must confess, being a lover of logical progressions and systems analysis can make it hard to keep that ideal straight. That is at least until I look into the eyes of someone in desperate need of answers to life's challenges and once again remember what the role of the church is really all about. As the truly great man of God, Dr. John Perkins recently reminded a room full of us at a Christian Community Development Association conference (as well as later in our personal meeting that same afternoon), "Nothing is more important than people." So the nagging question that should attach itself to every ministry is: *How does the manner in which we do church reflect God's purpose for the people we have been called to serve?*

This book is about a personal contribution I would like to make towards helping the churches, which are asking that very question, come to an understanding of what ministry is all about. More than merely inspiring individuals, I hope to inspire whole congregations to accept the challenge to become what I call "rational radicals" in their commitment not only to embracing the dynamic power of God for personal transformation, but also to inspiring a movement in the body of Christ to transform whole communities for His glory.

Our approach to ministry here at Bethel is one that seeks to empower our congregation to meet the challenges of 21st Century ministry. We seek to promote the kind of faith that moves the congregation from prayer, toward a level of performance that engages the broken, bruised and battered of our society in a manner that promotes spiritual, physical and social change. As a local ministry, we have accepted the divine call to become a church of God that says, "I do" to the Great Commission and its missional assignment—"To be the instrument of God's love to the World."

For too long the church has been engaged in recreational preaching that reveals an awareness of God's global agenda, but has failed to act in a committed manner that reflects and advances a dynamic change among the people whom we have been called to reach. At the risk of being accused of "church bashing", too much of what I see among too many of our church activities reflects a misguided quest to become a *mega church* rather than to aspire to the far more satisfying and loftier goal of embracing the *Mega God*.

Rather than attempt the sensational, I challenge you to read about a sincere but sound approach to ministry that glorifies our Savior and speaks to success. This book is intentionally written in an easy flowing style, sharing insights into how a relatively obscure church in Harlem, New York has evolved over time into a church that not only impacts upon its local community, but has found significant expression in several countries around the world.

Do I believe in the God of miracles? For many years, I have watched God do the miraculous through this church and through my life personally. Based on our experiences, I declare that it is not because of how special we are, but only by virtue of the incredible greatness of the God we serve that we have achieved the measure of accomplishment we have enjoyed. And I also declare to you that what God has done for us, He is all too willing and ready to do among others, regardless of the natural circumstances and based solely on the willingness to walk it out in faith.

Rev. Carlton Brown
New York City, 2008

1. THE RATIONAL RADICALS

ROMANS 12:1–2 says—

I beseech you therefore, brethren, by the mercies of God, that ye present your bodies a living sacrifice, holy, acceptable unto God, which is your reasonable service. And be not conformed to this world: but be ye transformed by the renewing of your mind, that ye may prove what is that good, and acceptable, and perfect, will of God.

On May 30, 1965, the late Vivian Juanita Malone Jones became the first black graduate of the University of Alabama. On June 11, 1963, she and James Hood, another black student, had to be escorted by federal troops through the doors of that university, in spite of the protestation of a racist Governor George Wallace, a hostile student body and crowd of onlookers, solely because of the color of their skin.

On the very next day, June 12, 1963, came the news that the Civil Rights activist Medgar Evers had been shot to death in Mississippi. Not long after, at about midnight, someone knocked on her dorm door telling her there was a bomb threat—one that did not materialize—but shortly afterward came three bomb blasts at the University, just four blocks from her dorm.

What was her response? The fact is that after Medgar Evers was killed she felt determined not to give up! She later shared, "I decided not to show any fear and went to classes that day!"

In 1996, out of respect for her courage and subsequent achievements in her field of study, the same Governor Wallace that had attempted to bar her entrance to the University of Alabama, proudly presented her with the Lurleen B. Wallace Award for Courage, named for his late wife. Just a few years before her death, Vivian Jones gave a speech and suggested one lesson that could be taken from her historic experience, simply stating: "You must always be ready to seize the moment." Wow. What awesome words of inspiration and admonishment!

At great odds, a young woman responded to an inner voice that directed her to face great danger to help release the destinies of the countless individuals who would follow her. As she faced the powerful forces that sought to restrict and deny her quest for higher education at this university, many well meaning voices urged her to accept things the way they were and seek the path of least resistance. *"Don't rock the boat,"* they urged as they struggled to understand why she was risking her very life for this cause.

By her own words, this young woman was not the type that sought to draw attention to herself, normally she would never have been considered a trouble maker. Yet she looked beyond the boundaries of her own comfort zone and caught a vision of what life could be for herself and others and took a bold step forward. While it was a path that some would view as *radical*, her vision perceived it as *rational* in the quest for justice and positive change.

What we need to recognize is that the church has long battled against a *DRTB* spirit within its ranks. This is what I call the *Don't Rock The Boat* strategy that works in the mind-set of some church boards and key individuals, frustrating the manner in which God would have our various assemblies define themselves. It is important that we understand that a *DRTB* approach to ministry will forever be inconsistent with and unsupportive of a healthy, God-ordained, Christ-centered approach to ministry. The church that hears and stands in the place established by God for His divine purpose must be a church that takes risks in the eyes of the world, one willing to make a statement towards the changing of the status quo.

It must be a people of God committed to being Rational Radicals! Here are some definitions to consider:

RATIONAL—having reason or understanding; or, relating to, based upon, or agreeable to reason.

RADICAL—indicating "more at the root"; also to be marked by a considerable departure from the usual or traditional; extreme—or, tending or disposed to make extreme changes in existing views, habits, conditions, or institutions.

I submit that in putting the two words together, we may describe a "Romans 12 individual" who is committed to furthering the will of God by whatever terms dictated through the freely expressed and experienced movement of the Holy Spirit. The problem with the church today is not the lack of availability of His presence, but the lack of receptivity of our leadership and congregational authorities to His leading. This is the evidence of the *DRTB spirit* at work in the midst of our congregation.

I have sometimes asked myself the question, *Why did God reach down to the most unlikely candidate and present us with a man like Paul to be such a dynamic teacher and example of His Will and purpose for the church?* After all, one could point out that this was a man responsible for the persecution of so many believers prior to his own conversion.

I believe that the answer is that Paul was just the kind of radical persona, radical but teachable, best suited to be used by God against the church's proclivity towards a DRTB strategy.

Paul, the rational radical of Acts 9:1–6, was a sincere man who was sincerely wrong! Up to this point Paul (Saul) was in fact involved in a radical (but rational to him) attempt to secure the Judaic passage on a type of "cruise to nowhere". Ignorant to the revelation of God and the revealed Messiah in the Lord Jesus Christ, Paul was committed to contain and systematically destroy the witness of the followers of the heretic Jesus of Nazareth. In that he was totally unaware that the present hope and destiny for creation had come, Paul was trying to lead from *the rabbinic understanding* of revelation according to old covenant law, ignorant of the truth of its fulfillment in the new covenant of peace that we now claim in Jesus Christ and promised by God through the prophets. Believing that he was stamping out the enemies of the authentic teachings of the Jewish faith, he came to terms with his error though a dynamic encounter with the risen Christ exclaiming—"Lord, what you will have me to do?"

Like Paul (Saul) of old, too many leaders in our churches of this day are guilty of leading from the *rear view mirror*—focusing on where we have *been* instead of being captivated by a Holy Spirit directive that focuses us on *where we are going*. The conservative and traditionalists of our churches insist on applying a 1950's approach to a 21st Century dynamic which falls short in addressing the fact that:

• We are confronted by a society that empowers so-called "gays" and denies the foundational truths of God's Word.

• We have been forced to witness the marginalization of inner city youth through the media glorification of a substandard reality that features Gangsta' rap, Gangsta' cars, super-sized Bling Bling, whorish appeal of young women and the proud display of turf war battle scars by our young men—even if self-inflicted.

• We have young girls in our communities starting their sexual experimentations as young as nine and ten-years old who proudly identify themselves as being "bisexual," "bi-curious," or just "gay".

• We have girls in the schools who are forcing young boys to engage in oral sex with them by threatening to spread rumors regarding their sexual orientation if they refuse.

• We have 60% of our black young men failing to graduate with a high school diploma—thus failing to make the grade in a high-tech-driven society.

• We gave in to the disowning of the poor and disenfranchised, despite a trillion dollar government mismanagement of our tax dollars and a zillion dollar tax-protected corporate machinery that plays the role of the "big bad wolf" by treating the consumers as sheep and by labeling its workers as expendable.

When on the road to Damascus, God radically transformed Paul's person and purpose, with the result that there was a complete turnaround in Paul's direction, but not in terms of the intensity of his commitment to those truths he perceived as divine truth. He understood the plight of the creation of God and the message that needed to be heard. No matter how drastically different his mission and message now appeared to others, and no matter the personal cost he now assumed in the relating of that message, Paul determined it to be the sole and rational course of action to proclaim that message to all people. Romans 12:1–2 establishes a position consistent with Galatians 2:20—

> *I am Crucified with Christ: nevertheless I live; yet not I, but Christ*
> *liveth in me: and the life which I now live I the flesh I live by the faith*
> *of the Son of God, who loved me, and gave himself for me.*

The rational ministry that is rooted in the Scriptures and the Holy Spirit will resort to radical means in order to establish what it understands to be an intrusive and practical solution to the onslaught of perversion and the rampant acts of injustice in our society. What may seem radical when your submarine commits to an emergency dive becomes totally rational when the periscope is up and focused upon the mines and depth charges ahead. The rational church will resort to radical means to establish what it understands to be the practical solution.

One principle idea that comes from the Romans 12 text is the *commitment to transformation*—"And be transformed by the renewing of your mind." Since the chapter further explores the ideal and personal commitment to the quality performance of the church's dedication to Divine

Purpose, it is vital that we attend to the idea of commitment to transformation.

When people ask me: "what is your vision?" I answer them in two words—

MORE GOD

Not satisfied? Then add two more words—

LESS FLESH!

Less self-centeredness	*Less* neediness
Less bitterness	*Less* excuses
Less woundedness	*Less* conceitedness

LESS US AND MORE CHRIST!

This is one of the principle messages that comes out of Romans 12. I believe that this text speaks to the effective and God-glorifying application of a Christ-centered life as expressed in our relationships with one another and the world at large. It speaks to the mind-set of a practicing Christian which qualifies the individual as a *rational radical.* The text reveals that this position can only be achieved and maintained through an intense worship of God, resulting in his promotion as a practical instrument in the hands of God. The rational radical is one who goes forward in faithful worship and service to God, as simply believing it to be "reasonable service."

Some time ago, I came across a statement by John Piper that never left me. In reference to the phrase reasonable service in Romans 12:2 he referred to it as "spiritual worship", meaning that before we give out we must lift up! What he said was: "Before Paul describes our new life in Christ as merciful he describes it as worshipful. Before you think that the Christian life has everything to do with being merciful to people, realize that it has everything to do with being worshipful toward God. 'I appeal to you therefore, brothers, by the mercies of God, to present your bodies as a living sacrifice, holy and acceptable to God, which is your spiritual worship.' Before we give ourselves away in mercy to man, we give ourselves away in worship to God." It is that level of worship that brings us to a rational radical approach in Christian life.

In early 2006, my Mission's Pastor and I traveled to a region of India where I had been asked to be a principal conference speaker. This particular ministry has been in existence for over forty years, and has been supported by Bethel for more than twenty years, as they faithfully planted seeds among the Hindus in an attempt to reach them for Jesus Christ. For the past ten years or more, for one reason or another, I was forced to decline their repeated invitations until this recent request, when we had received word on how one of the local ministers had been martyred for being a witness for Jesus.

The conference I was invited to would be the first major gathering of the local pastors and leaders since that event. Upon receiving this news, I heard the voice of God speak to me with a clear message: "This time you go!" There was nothing else for me to weigh or consider. Like ravenous dogs, the Hindu extremists in the area had the taste of blood dripping from their fangs, and the potential for a major confrontation was real.

Knowing the pressure upon that ministry, I understood the value that our physical presence could mean in this critical hour of their ministry. A stand had to be taken or the gain of forty years of sacrificial—and at times—physically painful ministry could be lost. If for nothing else, I wanted the leadership and workers to know that the church of America was standing with them—not from the comparatively safe location of our comfortable sanctuaries and freedom of religious expression, but on the very platform that had to have police protection as more than 40,000 people gathered to lift up a high praise to God in the middle of their spiritual stronghold.

I was blessed to preach on two separate occasions. On one particular night, we were warned that there were literally thousands of Hindu extremists surrounding the event, prepared to disrupt the meetings. Things were so dangerous our hosts had us locked up behind iron bars in our rooms, with instructions not to respond to any voice spoken through the door unless we recognized it to be one of their own.

Through all the dangers and threats, I was immeasurably blessed by what happened at that service. After preaching what others thought to be a strong spiritual warfare message, I was blessed to witness more than five hundred Hindus respond to our call to receive Jesus Christ as their Lord and Savior. As these men and women walked out into the open space between the platform and the crowd, I was humbled by the realization that in their rational decision to follow Jesus they had made a consciously radical choice to enter a world of familial and social persecution, all for the love of the God they had just come to know.

Yet, here is the thing. It only seemed radical to the physical mind's view. Just as in my own decision to risk danger in India, these individuals were now open and receptive to a fresh perspective fully informed by God. So real in its content and so comforting in its grasp, this act of conforming "by the renewing of your mind" may seem radical to the uninitiated, but it is a rational act that claims the fullness of life. What would have truly been radical at that moment would have been to deny the wooing, the sweet voice of the Spirit.

What I share is not to in any way lift up myself, or to suggest that putting one's life at risk is a simple act to achieve. What I desire to do in the chapters that follow is to testify to a reality of truth and a revelation of spiritual commitment and expression that can be achieved through worship. I will speak to the results that are attainable through a rational radical commitment to the voice of the Holy Spirit.

In the coming chapters, I will offer the background and tell the stories of the significant leaders of the church who helped to form this measure of commitment in my life. I will share the experiences that testify to the transformative power of God to do significant work in life after life, ministry after ministry, resulting in radical change around the world. Finally, I will suggest ideas and structures that will facilitate healthy expressions that will not only make disciples, but raise up a credible witness in communities that are hungry for a gospel that brings both deliverance and final victory.

It is time that the church enter the Sunday morning experience not with the intention of having church, but consumed with the flaming desire to be the church—the church that God had in mind from the beginning.

It is time for the church of the Lord Jesus Christ to "seize the moment."

It is time to be rational radicals for Christ!

2. 'TIL DEATH DO WE S.H.O.P.!

It has often been said that you cannot accurately determine where you are going if you are ignorant of where you came from.

Harlem, USA! Uptown Manhattan! A name that evokes inspiring yet conflicting, and in some cases, frightening images in the minds of the masses of people, depending on their knowledge of this, the most famous village in what is arguably the greatest city in the world. It is a place rich in history: President Grant is buried here. Fidel Castro set up temporary headquarters here. Duke Ellington and Josephine Baker performed here. The legendary Cotton Club swayed here. Malcolm reigned here and Martin prophesied here, while Adam Clayton Powell Jr. worked, prayed, and played here! Daddy Grace and Father Divine ruled their kingdoms here. Mother Horn delivered here. W.E.B. DuBois and Marcus Garvey dissented and disagreed here! The Apollo Theater entertains here. At the turn of the last century, Black people felt safe here. In 1917, Bethel Gospel Assembly was born here. (Rev. Carlton T. Brown)

During a recent and rare two-man shopping excursion undertaken by me and my then twenty-year-old son, Justin, we heard those fateful words that have dashed the hopes of many a brave bargain-hunting soul at the end of a shoppers' paradise extravaganza—

"Attention shoppers, this store is now closing. Please bring
your purchases to the nearest cashier for checkout!"

Like most men, Justin and I tend to shop only out of sheer necessity, but on the eve of our family cruise there were a few last minute items we needed. With only forty-five minutes to spare, we raced up to the Burlington Coat Factory on a Saturday night just half an hour before closing to do our "man thing" (You know, flag it, tag it and bag it).

This time I thought we might have cut the time too close, owing to the wide selection of outstanding bargains available (it was a particularly good hunting safari). We were hoping to get all of our work done before the fateful words came over the loud speaker, forcing us to call an end to the hunt and leave with too many bargains left on the table, for God only knew when we would pass that way again. It was not a nice feeling.

Yet, in truth, we were only talking about a few items of clothing that would have been barely missed once our laundry was done. What was the big deal? More important was that the signal that we received in the store that night reminded me of this project, particularly the critical piece designed to describe, in associative language, who we really are as a collective body of believers in the Kingdom of the Lord. In addressing the new believers and members coming into our church, I felt the need to present a detailed and heartfelt message as to who they are in reality, particularly within this new life they have come to embrace.

Over and above the many terminologies, scriptural language, "do's and don'ts", and code names that are about to inundate the reader, I felt it important to share the heart and soul of who we are as believers in a manner that would remain with you forever. I wanted to shrink all of the religious jargon and concepts into a user-friendly expression that would sum up our identity in relation to the One who called us and transforms our lives, as well as inspires us to be "steadfast, unmovable and always abounding" in His service.

The term that stuck with me is a simple and common concept: "Shop". This is a word that attaches itself to us in many different ways. Whether we like to shop or not, shopping is a reality that none of us can do without. We shop for food, clothes and shelter—all necessities for survival. We shop for girlfriends, boyfriends and, eventually, husbands and wives. We shop for furniture, cars, houses and even churches. And all of us shop for bargains, even if it is something we do not really need.

It may seem awkward to place our Lord Jesus Christ in the same mundane categories that we put ourselves, but the truth is that He is a shopper as well. In Luke 19:10 the Bible states, "For the Son of man is come to seek and to save that which was lost." We are led to understand that the process of His attaining ownership of the lost came through the shedding of His own blood—thereby "redeeming" us at great cost from the hand of Satan by purchasing us from sin, judgment and death. As illustrated by the enslaved Black peoples in America a century and a half ago, all humanity are bound in chains as slaves. It is Christ who came to deliver us from the cruel hands of our slave master into the freedom land of the Divine Kingdom of God.

When framed in this way, we can add a more in-depth picture to the shopper's instinct inside all of us which is now handed over and used by God for His purpose. Not only do we successfully gain access to the greatest bargain one can ever attain, our submission to the purchase transaction of Christ through the Cross of Calvary, but now, as sons of God, we are led by our Savior in the greatest shopping expedition ever. We witness and participate in the saving of souls from the hand of the enemy, being constantly aware that the horn may sound at any moment, calling us to the spiritual register at check-out time, where those purchased by the saving work of the Lord Jesus are packaged and carried home to meet their Savior.

In Part II of this book I will provide a breakdown of S.H.O.P as it applies to the development of a focused ministry that stands in compliance with the Biblical mandate. It is my hope that you will refrain from skipping forward, and rather allow the text to flow, leading you progressively in the context of the overall message provided.

While this study outlines the historical, philosophical and strategic formation that describes the uniqueness of the ministry at Bethel Gospel Assembly located in Harlem, New York, the reader will also be directed toward the critical elements giving rise to spiritual movements impacting our world today.

This book is written to tell the story to the Christian community of the impact of Christ's purchase upon two young souls nearly one hundred years ago. This episode in the Lord's triumphant shopping expedition not only resulted in establishing Bethel Gospel Assembly as a positive force within a much maligned and abused Harlem, but also subsequently propelled and empowered the same body of believers to boldly project the redemptive love of Christ throughout the world. In later chapters, we will reflect together upon our ministry campaigns to such places as Cuba, the forgotten people in the mountains of Venezuela, and such places as Albania and (for security reasons) an unnamed Muslim nation where we were able to share the powerful witness of Christ.

As I add these places to the list of nations with which we have ministry connections in Africa, the Caribbean, as well as the nation of India, you will witness our commitment to the Great Commission, as well as to God's faithfulness to every body of believers who will say, "Here am I, send me."

Also we will share how the same understanding of the divine purpose of the church led to the acquisition and renovation of a four-story 167,000-square-foot property in the middle of Harlem. You will see how in 1982, through the faithful giving of less than two hundred tithe-paying members of modest income, God raised up a "spiritual hospital in Harlem" where the Word is demonstrated in a display of power that transforms the lives of men and women!

This is not another one of those, "How To" books, although we do believe that the principles and standards outlined in this work are applicable to any and every body of believers. It is my greater desire to escort you through an inspirational and informative excursion describing how God continues to use His children in extraordinary ways. It is important to bear in mind that these works are accomplished even as we submit to His process and principles in each unique situation.

The signs of the times tell us that the Kingdom of God is at hand. In light of the season and the great demand of the Lord's harvest, and true to the calling of every great bargain hunter out there, we have no other recourse but to "shop till we drop," or in the spirit of the marriage covenant, 'Til Death Do We S.H.O.P.! Selah.

PART I
THE SPIRIT OF THINGS TO COME
THE FOUNDING OF A MINISTRY

The next two chapters will take you on a brief historical journey highlighting some of the key events that shaped Bethel Gospel Assembly and gave rise to the S.H.O.P. model that is the driving concept of both our ministry and this book. The information provided here will help the reader visualize the principles outlined in the book, as well as to identify ways this model can be adapted to your own particular ministry. You may be tempted to move along to Part II, and if that is your choice, the information provided there will be a blessing to you. However, we strongly urge you to take time to read the unique story of Bethel's origin. At the very least, the chapters in Part I will present a wonderful view of the miracle-working power of God, providing inspiration and encouragement to you as you face your own particular set of challenges.

Bethel Gospel Assembly Building

The Inscription on Bethel Gospel Assembly Building

3. NOT EXACTLY ORDINARY

In the late 1960s and '70s, Black gospel music underwent an evolutionary shift in musical style and lyrics. While the driving musical force of the choir, edged on by the power of the Leslie speaker, will most likely endure until the end of time, this was the era of the intricate melodies and thoughtful, moving lyrics of Andre Crouch, Edwin and Walter Hawkins, and, of course, the late Dannibelle Hall. It was in the late Eighties when, as youth leader at Bethel, I brought in the gifted and talented Dannibelle to be the featured guest at our first major youth conference at our new facility. Humble and sweet, she graciously commanded the stage and the hearts of all of us that night, sharing through verse and melody the goodness and faithfulness of God.

With great anticipation, the audience heard the opening strains of her signature song, *Ordinary People*. You could feel the strong identification of the young African-American audience with the artist and her song. Recognizing it to be more than a catchy tune with sensitive words, this song was an anthem to every soul that has run the gauntlet of experience and emotion common to those who have often heard the words, "Not good enough!" You could sense the collective exhalation of relief and the swelling renewal of hope within the audience as she sang those reassuring words, *"Little becomes much when we place it in the Master's hand."*

The truth is every picture *does* tell a story, and there is nothing ordinary in the telling of the tales of our lives. Rather than being ordinary, our personal testimonies are colored by accounts of disappointment, rejection, abuse, failure, brutality, loneliness and isolation, woven into so many combinations that no one could describe them as merely ordinary!

The popular inclination is to take the sum total of those circumstances, and then judge the final product of our lives as adding up to what is ordinary. Yet the message of the song reveals the secret ingredient that adds "that little something extra" to the equation. What drove one little lad to follow the crowd's movement toward Jesus Christ? What combination of hope and despair led him to offer up his "poor man's lunch", in the belief that it could help to feed several thousand men, women and children? (John 6:8–10)

Whatever the young lad's specific condition, his actions unlocked for us a tremendous and liberating truth that has endured the trials of time. The little lad has become a shining example for every man and woman driven by faith as they learn that their ordinary condition can become extraordinary when they express the faith and courage to place their love and sacrifice in the hands of our Master and Savior Jesus Christ.

The Prophet Isaiah (53:5) reveals God's understanding of our human condition as revealed through the words, "But He was wounded for our transgressions, bruised for our iniquities: the chastisement of our peace was upon Him; and with His stripes we are healed." The pain of our suffering and the darkening of our understanding are taken into account as the Savior presents Himself willing and efficient in the transformation of the bruised, the broken and the bound.

Whether we are the products of a dysfunctional home environment, the emotional and physical sufferers of sexual abuse, or the victims of oppressive spiritual and social systems, the Jesus that we preach and represent brings hope through the demonstration of transformation. He is real and His words are true, not just because I tell you so, but because I show you it is true from Scripture! This is the kind of presentation that changes lives as I have witnessed in cities of this nation such as Harlem and Dallas and in the nations of Venezuela, India and beyond.

Jesus declared in Luke 4:18–19—

The Spirit of the Lord is upon Me, Because He has anointed Me to preach the gospel to the poor; He has sent Me to heal the brokenhearted. To proclaim liberty to the captives and recovery of sight to the blind. To set at liberty those who are oppressed; To proclaim the acceptable year of the Lord. (NKJV)

One of many powerful accounts of God's power to transform comes from the life of someone we have been blessed to know here at Bethel. His life story presents a life that was far from ordinary. In my forthcoming book, *MP3: Men of Purpose, Passion and Promise,* I share the following account of a wonderful man of God—

A man who has played a significant role in Bethel's ministry was Reverend Walter Wilson. Walter grew up in Harlem in the days when it was notorious all over the world for its strange brew of mystery and intrigue, crime and passion, poverty and destruction. Walter's life was typical of the mean streets of the Fifties through the Seventies. A small boy who once had to run for cover to survive, he grew in stature until he dominated the community that shaped him. Rough and tough, lean and mean, Walter's name evoked fear in his enemies and accolades from his friends. A thoughtful man, he used his time in prison to retreat from the street, review the situation and tighten his grip on the Harlem underworld. Utilizing all his God-given intellect and leadership skills, Walter thought he had it all, until he came upon a book that showed him that, in reality, all that his assets amounted to was a firm hold on death.

After a police raid stripped one of his strongholds bare, Walter was amazed to find laying at his feet the one thing they had left behind, a Bible. Compelled by the Holy Spirit, he read and read and read some more, until he had read the Good Book from cover to cover. Then and there, through reading of the Word of God, the Holy Spirit filled Walter with God's love and he surrendered his heart to the Lord.

Turning his back on everything that he had built by his own daring and expertise, he began a faith walk that has been an inspiration to men and women wherever he has been led by God. Submitting all of his gifts and talents to God, he completed college and led the Beth Hark Counseling Center for over fifteen years at Bethel Gospel Assembly.

Walter brought all to the cross to follow Jesus. In doing so there is one key thing that this tough guy did not leave behind. He brought his passion. The same passion he once reserved for fame and gain, he surrendered to Christ, and, with the same verve and vigor that he once used to bust hell wide open, he now proclaims the name and fame of Jesus. Today, as a much sought after speaker, sometimes with cheers and sometimes with tears, he is not ashamed of the Gospel of Jesus Christ even as he offers the power of salvation to everyone who believes through the preaching of the word.

ROMANS 1:16 says—

For I am not ashamed of this Good News about Jesus Christ. It is the power of God at work, saving everyone who believes... (NLT)

Today, Walter Wilson's zeal for the things of the world has been surpassed by a greater passion centered in knowing and walking within God's will. He is not an ordinary product of the mean streets of Harlem, but an extraordinary model of what one can become through God's grace.

This account and others like it testify to the dynamic power of God to bring about dramatic change in the lives of those who submit to His divine truth. The transforming nature of this personal relationship with God is not specific to any race or religious denomination, but is consistent throughout communities that exercise faith built upon a Biblical foundation exercised through spiritual immersion in the truth of the Holy Spirit. What needs to be revived in our church and home communities is the reality that beautiful, wonderful things can actually happen outside of the imagination of movie-maker Stephen Spielberg. The shackles of our past, the dubiousness of our present, and the cloudiness of our future can all be swallowed up in a spiritual whirlwind of reformation, and we can be changed. I have staked my life on that truth and have yet to be proven wrong.

You may ask, "Where does such confidence come from?" The next chapter will shed light as to the origins of our faith.

Lillian Kraeger
Bethel's Founder

Bethel in the 1940s

Mortgage Burning in 1965

4. DEFINITELY SOMETHING EXTRAORDINARY
BETHEL'S BEGINNINGS

To effectively convey to you our confidence in our ability to make a difference in the face of such global indifference, it is important to present a broad overview of the history of our church. Our purpose is not to boast about ourselves, but to boast about our God in the hope of boosting all of us in our faith in God, a God who is able to do the extraordinary in our lives. In this sense our history is hardly unique—it is a common description of the workings of the mighty God we serve. As a church born out of rejection, yet brimming with courage and humility, each of these elements have come to be identified as trademarks of this ministry over the ninety-plus years of our existence.

PSALM 84: 1–4 says—
(1) *How amiable are thy tabernacles, O LORD of hosts!*
(2) *My soul longeth, yea, even fainteth for the courts of the LORD: my heart and my flesh crieth out for the living God.*
(3) *Yea, the sparrow hath found an house, and the swallow a nest for herself, where she may lay her young, even thine altars, O LORD of hosts, my King, and my God.*
(4) *Blessed are they that dwell in thy house: they will be still praising thee. Selah.*

As we look into the history of Bethel our attention is drawn to two key realities:

First, we remember and celebrate those who came before us. As stated in Psalm 84, there is reference to a people that found something awesome and refreshing in the house of the Lord, even as they remained in fellowship with Him. The text uses the images of birds that find their location so secure and accommodating that they build their nests to have their young. In this passage the psalmist was referring to the habit of birds actually to nest in the temple. The psalmist indicates the immutability of the Lord and thereby we find the enduring nature of worship among those in fellowship, as the psalmist declares perpetual praise with the passage of time, "They will be still praising Thee…"

I find this passage to be a wonderful testimony to the faith of our forebears, as they found their fellowship with God to be an awe-inspiring experience that meant more to them than what the entire world had to offer, as with great faithfulness they shared this witness with us. Even as we have "nestled" in our understanding of what they proved God to be during these many years, we are still here praising Him for who He is and what He has done!

Second, as each succeeding generation of Bethel faces its share of challenges, we find that the same God and the same faith that brought our fathers through their wilderness, works in us to the same measure as well. Jesus proves Himself to be all that we heard Him to be, and so much more because we are learning to prove Him for ourselves. We can say, "Jesus, the same yesterday and today—know His truth forever!"

In truth one might recognize that Bethel is a war baby. There is an old saying, "The more things change, the more they remain the same." Even as this present time finds our nation and the world facing the threat of terrorism, back in 1916 the world was dealing with what was, for them, equally unimaginable, as they battled against tyrannical forces in the so-called "Great War." It came to be called "The War to End all Wars," so horrific was its nature and impact. The conflict was so grave that it forced President Wilson of the United States to go back on his pledge of neutrality and cast America's lot with the allied forces fighting in Europe. After the sinking of the *Lusitania* by a German U-boat and the decoding of a secret German message (the Zimmerman Telegram), uncovered by British secret agents urging Mexico to attack the United States, Congress declared war on Germany on April 6, 1917.

World War I became a proving ground for governments to test new weapons designed to kill more efficiently than those of their adversaries. New war machines, such as the airplane, the submarine or U-boat—which was used by the Germans to challenge Britain's sea power, British tanks and the machine gun made World War I the bloodiest and costliest conflict up to that time. The clash between opposing forces resulted in the deaths of over twenty million men, women and children, and the expenditure of $300 billion dollars to win a victory that left both the victor and the vanquished exhausted and dissatisfied with the final result.

It was in the midst of all this confusion that a very special movement was born. While the war against aggression was being fought in Europe, an individual of Germanic extraction was fighting another war in New York City. This was a very personal war against racism and white Christian bigotry. It was a battle being fought by a young German-American woman, Lillian Kraeger, who stood up against the ignorance of her times and allowed the Holy Spirit to use her to speak to two black girls and their friends in Harlem.

As quoted from our Fiftieth Anniversary Journal, the late May Allison, a longstanding mother in our church and one of the principles involved, said: "Two black girls applied for membership at a white church in the downtown area, but they were refused admission because of their color. This rejection grieved them greatly, but it was in the plan of the Master, for that closed door redirected their steps to an entrance through which hundreds were to be led to a saving knowledge of Jesus Christ." Mother May went on to say, "Lillian Kraeger (a young woman of German descent) heard our plight and suggested that we have cottage meetings."

"Lillian Kraeger committed herself to teaching them the Bible, if they were willing to bring their friends to the sessions. This was in January 1916, and while it cost her wedding engagement, she believed she'd heard from God and fearlessly journeyed to Harlem. As a direct result of her faithful submission to God's will, on November 18th, 1917 at 11:00 AM, Bethel Gospel Assembly was born."

It should be noted that this event took place roughly ten years after the Pentecostal movement began. It is speculated that part of Lillian Kraeger's sense of urgency to come to Harlem was to insure that the Pentecostal legacy continued through the conversion of these two young girls, not being sure of the existence of other Pentecostal churches in the Harlem community at that time.

Born in the gutter of rejection and adversity, the church's growth mirrored the images that surrounded her. In a few short years, Harlem emerged into a legendary period of notoriety and prosperity. The Roaring Twenties were a wonderful time to sample the life of Uptown as tremendous numbers of socialites and their upper crust associates came to Harlem to share in the exciting night life of its cafés, bars and clubs, and to listen to and rub shoulders with her jazz and literary greats. Important African American writers of the time included Sterling A. Brown, James Weldon Johnson, Countee Cullen, Langston Hughes, Claude McKay, Jean Toomer, Jesse Redmon Fauset and Zora Neale Hurston.

Bethel also thrived as the church grew in size, strength and vision, becoming a true mission church by supporting the transplanting of Reverend and Sister Kenneth Spooner, a black couple, to their Spirit-appointed destination—South Africa. A few years later, Bethel launched the support of Venus Williams in her church-planting endeavors on the small Island of St. Vincent.

By 1923, with $5,000.00 in the bank, Bethel moved to purchase a private house located at 255 West 131st Street, and by 1924, Bethel was duly organized, incorporated and registered in the City of New York, equipped with a mandate from God and a willingness to serve.

Now, at the turn of the 21st Century, Harlem is going through a startling renaissance. Even the former President of the United States, Bill Clinton, found the area desirable enough to set up his private office in its very heart on 125th Street. Property values continue to soar as new buildings spring up in areas that had been an eyesore to residents, particularly those who could remember the happier times of yesteryear. In the center of these events, Bethel continues to thrive and continues to praise God for His manifold blessings, as the Lord has anointed this ministry to be a continuing source of hope to this community and beyond.

Ninety years after the birth of Bethel, we are once again facing global conflict on a scale never before witnessed by man. The "War on Terror" has already cost hundreds of billions of dollars, and only time will reveal the numbers of casualties it will cause. President George W. Bush has vowed to pursue this war until every terrorist threat in the world has been eliminated, but the war we are fighting is different from previous wars, for not only is the enemy scattered in many nations, among friend and foe alike, but also exists as an invisible but lethal threat on this very soil.

HE ATTENDED P.S. 120
NOW HE OWNS IT··

Bishop Ezra Williams outside current building

It couldn't have been said better. "Too often we come with just the gospel." Those are the words of Rev. Ezra Williams, pastor of the Bethel Gospel Assembly, a Pentecostal church on 123rd Street and Lenox Avenue in Harlem.

Bethel just plunked down $300,000 to take possession of P.S. 120, once a famous junior high school in Harlem that was popularly known as "Cooper." And they're going to do all kinds of things there to make, as Rev. Williams stated, "a missionary contribution to the community."

The church will move into the building so that the 350-400 members will have more room to conduct services. But it goes past worship. Plans are to have a crisis center to help solve family disputes. They'll give out food and clothing to the needy. They are researching the possibilities of a day care center on the premises. Residential space is set aside for folks who ⬛ drug addi ⬛ place to st ⬛

Recreati ⬛ youth will ⬛ in the sch ⬛ first gradu ⬛ Harlem be ⬛ munity. H ⬛ Bethel Go ⬛ years. W ⬛ Cooper, it ⬛

Photo by Dennis Smith

A New Day in Bethel History--Bishops Williams and Brown break ground on the new complex

Bishop Brown and Elder Lorna Brown at the complex ground breaking, 2006

Construction of new facility is well underway

5. THE LOVING, LEARNING AND LAUNCHING CHURCH

"How did I get into a mess like this?" I asked myself in the spring of 1986 while sitting with very little money in my pocket at the cargo area exit of the Murtala Muhammed Airport in Lagos, Nigeria, about 9,000 miles from home.

Let me go back a bit. Under the leadership of my pastor, Bishop Ezra N. Williams, and my missions director, Dr. Ruth Onukwue, I was chosen to be a conference speaker for the Family Circle Ministry's spring conference in Enugu, Nigeria. The Family Circle Ministry continues to be a multimedia networking force in Nigeria, specializing in the building of strong families. We had supported them for several years, and at that point, as one of the Associate Pastor's of Bethel, I'd been asked to spend two weeks traveling to several states in Nigeria, speaking on the topic of marriage and family.

There was one other small matter. To further our support to this ministry, we had purchased a very valuable and essential piece of equipment for their printing press. To ensure that it reached its destination, it was decided that we would send it with a guarantee it would arrive in time for me to sign for it and deliver it personally. You guessed it: I arrived on time and our precious cargo did not! As it turned out, it was a good thing it was not there!

The cargo was not there, but the Family Circle Ministry representatives were, and they collected my travel companion and me without our cargo and loaded us up in the cargo truck they had supplied and we began our seven-plus hour drive to Family Circle Ministry headquarters. Nothing had prepared me for what happened next!

Shortly after pulling out, we found ourselves stopped, searched and seized by men in uniform allegedly in search of some kind of contraband (mind you, all of this took place around midnight). Just before reaching their headquarters, they pulled our little convoy over into a dark alley and demanded a bribe in order to keep us out of jail. Our host's representative made a unilateral decision to pay a sizable amount of money for our release, only to realize that we had nothing of real value in our possession. I was just beginning to perceive the challenges that lay ahead.

We got back on the road that same night and continued our journey to Ministry headquarters. As tired as I was, before long I fell asleep, although I still had the presence of mind to note that our vehicle had been stopped and searched at least twelve times on the way to Enugu. These searches were conducted by armed guards, members of the police and military personnel checking our vehicles for anything valuable enough to warrant a bribe. But since we had nothing of value, they let us pass. Praise the Lord, we arrived without serious incident. After a warm reception, we proceeded to have a powerful time in ministry and saw God moving in miraculous ways with healings and breakthroughs against demonic strongholds. But for me, the greatest miracle was about to take place.

The following week, word came that our cargo was on the way from Amsterdam. It was decided that I would go back with a Family Circle Ministry representative and driver to pick up the package. We arrived at the airport, but could not get assistance to locate our cargo before it closed for the night. Then God began a miraculous process that would change my life forever.

God caused us to meet someone who not only knew our ministry, but also happened to be the agent required to negotiate the pickup of all cargo. Checking his sources, he located our package in customs, but informed us that it was too late for us to pick it up that night. He told us to come back in the morning to begin the process. He also told us to be prepared to pay large bribes just to get the customs people to talk to us, let alone assist us. That was the last thing I needed to hear.

Trusting God, we returned to his office in the morning, but the agent never showed up. At four in the afternoon I was praying what to do next, when the Lord told me to turn to Jeremiah 32. Reading from the portion where Jeremiah handed over the documents, I continued to the blessed phrase in Verse 37, "Behold, I am the Lord, the God of all flesh, is there anything too hard for me?" I had barely said "Amen" when my companion from Family Circle Ministry turned to me and said, "It's getting late. I want to at least see what we are dealing with. You wait here while I go in. Give me your documents of ownership." At this point I did not know who to trust in Nigeria, but the Lord brought back to me the portion that read, "When he handed him the documents." I said a silent prayer and put the documents into the hands of this relative stranger and watched him disappear into the mass of humanity on the streets. My fear said to me, "At least you have your plane ticket on you to get a flight home," but faith answered fear and said, "I trust God."

An hour later, the agent who had promised to help us came running into his office offering apologies, telling me because of the lateness of the hour we would have to try again tomorrow. He suddenly stopped and asked, "Where's your friend?" That was a good question because the place had closed half an hour before the man walked through the door. Almost as if on cue, my companion bolted through the door, with the documents flashing in his hand. With a wide grin on his face, he announced to everyone in the room, "It's finished!" The agent blurted out, grabbing the documents out of his hand, "What do you mean, 'it's finished?'"

He explained that all the required stamps and orders of transfer had been secured. With a perplexed look on his face, our agent nodded his head slowly in agreement. "Yes, you're right! It's all here. How on earth did you accomplish in such a short time what would've taken me, with all my expertise, at least half the day to accomplish?"

Suddenly, his eyes narrowed and he asked, "How much did you have to pay?" Great question, my empty pockets and I thought as we waited for my companion's response. "It was just a few dollars" he replied, still grinning. Bewildered but satisfied, the agent returned the freshly stamped documents to me and said, "It's done. Your friend did a better job than I could have. Since I did nothing, there's no charge."

He was wrong, he did do something important; he gave me a chance to begin to learn the love of God in a more direct, intimate fashion. I saw God work through my dire circumstances in my loneliest season to build my faith up to a new and greater level as I launched out in Christ. I thought the agent was going to be our answer, when the truth was that God Himself was going to do it.

Since we could not pick up our cargo due to the late hour, we went back to our hotel where my new friend in Christ described what happened when he went to the customs office. On at least four occasions he was rudely received by arrogant, sometimes shady officials, some of them Muslims, who did not want to help him because our documents identified us as being Christian.

He said that after each encounter, he went to a nearby spot and simply prayed. Then, miraculously and without explanation, the officials came out of their offices, took the documents from his hands and signed for the release of the cargo without any of the expected bribes that are a way of life for these underpaid civil servants. All he had to pay were the standard fees for the stamps, a nominal charge. Praise God!

That is exactly what I did that night, but in the morning I found myself looking for the promised joy all over again. Having picked up the package, all I could see was a traffic officer purposely holding us up at the gate as he allowed for all of the oncoming traffic to pass. Our driver said to no one in particular, "He's waiting for his cut on the cargo," and I thought to myself, "Him, and all twelve checkpoints we passed through on our way to Enugu." At that point my companion jumped out of the truck, taking some Family Circle Ministry pamphlets with him. Walking up to the officer, he politely handed them to him and said, "God Bless you." The officer glanced down at the material, nodded his head, stopped the flow of oncoming traffic and let us pass.

I quietly said to myself, "I got it, Lord!" And then in a loud voice I took hold of the spiritual authority that He had given us over the situation by declaring, "Lord, cover the eyes of the soldiers at all the checkpoints along our path. Secure us so that they will not interfere with your servants as we carry out your mission on this day."

Our faith in place, we proceeded on our nine-hour journey. Wide awake, I was excited to watch how God continued to work on our behalf, and He did just that. I counted twenty checkpoints on our way back to our ministry headquarters. Men with guns in hand were pulling cars off the road left and right, but only two tried to stop us.

The first officer actually got us to stop, but once we handed him a couple of *Family Circle* magazines, he let us go without searching the truck. The second officer tried to stop us while we were driving at forty-five miles an hour. Waving us towards the side of the road, he made his intentions clear. I said to myself, "This can't be happening. Lord, you have to do something." Just then a large open truck filled with hay, driving fast, shot past on our left and jumped in front of us, then hit the brakes and drove straight toward the checkpoint, ignoring the frantic efforts of the officer indicating that it was not his but our truck that he wanted!

Our driver saw his chance, hit the gas and moved into the left lane, pretending he'd never seen the officer's summons. With a triumphant smile on my face, I watched out the corner of my eye as the defeated officer waved his hand at us in disgust as he turned to hurl abuse at our angel of grace.

When Satan has you in a mess, it is important to remember that God is just getting ready to bless. The full implications of this incredible facet of our spiritual existence is never lost on the people of God who understand that He is looking for a church that is loving, learning and launching.

The Bethel that I am privileged to lead today is multi-ethnic, although mostly African-American in its makeup. It is based in a changing Harlem, populated by people of all racial, economic and educational levels. As a church of color, we believe it is essential that we both exemplify and share with the larger Christian community the mandate given by Christ to every believer. We believe in the power of God to transform entire communities and have committed ourselves to doing just that.

At the beginning of my assignment as Senior Pastor, it was important to emphasize the essentials of ministry as taught to me through the ministry of the great man that came before me, Bishop Ezra N. Williams. As a church with a heart for the lost, and through tremendous lessons learned through scripture, we teach the believer to understand the faith community as:

A Loving Church—Each is important.
A Learning Church—Each is improving.
A Launching Church—Each is impacting.

Just as perception is a great lead-in to realizing purpose, so love is a major facilitator in learning. It is no accident that the courses we learned best in our school days were those we loved! In the same way, as we lock in on the love of God there is an impetus to learn the ways of God! (see Deuteronomy 6:4–5.)

St. Augustine said, "Love God, then do as you please." If we love God enough to want to do what is pleasing in His sight, then we need never worry about our conduct because the things that will not please God will not please us either. If we lack love for God, all the rules in the world will not keep us true to Him. The law tells us what to do; love gives the power to do it.

Love is not a part-time affair, but a full-time occupation (possession) in constant need of upgrading and maintenance! If I am sick, don't give me a part-time doctor. Give me someone who loves his occupation so much that his idea of a perfect evening is reading about the latest findings in the *American Journal of Medicine*! Bringing passion to the matter at hand is essential to excellence. Love seeks out a greater knowledge of its heart's desire, and the knowledge we receive moves us to share with others by launching out.

God's Church is a launching church—each impacting! We see examples of this in Acts 2:43–47, where the church added to its numbers daily through its loving and learning relationships. We also find another example in I Thessalonians 1:6–8, where the church's labor of love results in its message being carried abroad, where others get the chance to learn about its steadfast hope in God. We understand the launching church must be continually fueled by the power of the Holy Ghost!

Having the distinct pleasure to have been raised in Bethel since birth, it has been my great honor and opportunity to witness the ascendancy of Ezra N. Williams, first to the pastorate, and then later to the position of a national bishop. Sitting beneath his powerful teaching on love and learning the way that God revealed Himself to him from his youth, inspired me and countless others to develop a kindred passion for the intimacy of God. His counsel throughout my formative years has played a key part in preparation for service at this time, giving me the courage to launch out into missions and ministry regardless of the challenges. Bishop Williams has been a wonderful spiritual father to my wife Lorna and me. While he has retired from the front lines of service, he continues to be a lasting inspiration for all that we do at Bethel Gospel Assembly today.

On December 7, 1999, Bishop Williams presented me before the assembled membership of Bethel Gospel Assembly as the one to succeed him as the Senior Pastor and Chairman of the Board of Bethel Gospel Assembly, Inc. By pledged agreement of the Assembly, and with my wife Lorna at my side, I was installed as Senior Pastor on the fourth Sunday of

February, 2000.

In 2001, God gave us an affirmation for each member to rehearse, to recognize His call to excellence as a child of God. Based on the scriptures found in Romans 12:1–2, these words were given to me early one morning:

> I am accountable.
> I am correctable.
> I am transformable.
> Presenting myself a living sacrifice to God.
> By the love of God.
> By the Word of God.
> By the grace of God.
> Completely supplied in Christ Jesus.
> Unto all good works.

Now simply entitled "Bethel's Affirmation," this statement inspires us and reminds us of our purpose as believers. That in this "Loving, Learning and Launching" environment we can realize lives that are transformed to be effective for the building up of godly communities everywhere we go.

At the core of these words exist the philosophy of our ministry expressed through S.H.O.P.! The next chapter explains this concept in greater detail and presents a viable model that will help propel ministries toward an acceptable and balanced presentation of the Word of God as it lives through His church.

PART II

LET'S TALK S.H.O.P.

SEEKERS OF THE BLESSED HOPE,
ORDAINED FOR DIVINE PURPOSE!

UNDERSTANDING THE PHILOSOPHY OF MINISTRY

TITUS 2:11-15 says—

(11) *For the grace of God that bringeth salvation hath appeared to all men,*

(12) *Teaching us that, denying ungodliness and worldly lusts, we should live soberly, righteously, and godly, in this present world;*

(13) *Looking for that blessed hope, and the glorious appearing of the great God and our Saviour Jesus Christ;*

(14) *Who gave himself for us, that he might redeem us from all iniquity, and purify unto himself a peculiar people, zealous of good works.*

(15) *These things speak, and exhort, and rebuke with all authority, Let not man despise thee.*

It was in 1964 at the age of ten that the intricacies of the game of baseball began to unfold for me. My favorite team was the New York Yankees, and my passion for reading took me to the public library where I found a book titled, *The History of the American League.* I was treated to the statistics and stories of some of the greatest teams and players in the history of the game, and it was clear in my ten-year-old mind that baseball was indeed America's favorite sport.

39

Of course, in time that notion was to undergo a tremendous adjustment. As an African-American youth, I soon learned that the National League ran slightly ahead of its counterpart in recruiting black and Latino players, with, I might add, my beloved Yankees trailing behind most teams in that regard. Some of the greatest players that ever played the game were denied the opportunity to display their talents before the masses and were relegated to substandard fields and smaller venues around the country.

Then, as the overall pace of the game continued to slow to a crawl, the imagination and passion for life in America continued to accelerate, making the perpetual motion of basketball and the explosiveness of football far more appealing to the youth of this impatient country.

Yet the basic elements of the game of baseball continue to offer us a splendid model for the achievement of corporate goals. Despite the increasingly selfish mind-set of many of today's sports heroes, the game of baseball remains a team sport, filled with images that lend themselves to a spiritual application. Terms such as "save" and "sacrifice" (whether by a bunt or a fly ball) are as applicable to a Sunday morning service as they are to a lazy summer Sunday afternoon in the bleachers of your favorite ballpark.

The term "home run" has become a mainstay in our vocabulary, as easily used to describe a decisive victory by a lawyer in a courtroom as the slugging feats of baseball great Barry Bonds, or the effectiveness of a great sermon delivered by your favorite preacher.

The most compelling analogy stems from the strategy of the game itself, which is to get runners on base and then get them home. I believe this view very neatly sums up the believer's quest in life, and hence we have used the familiar image of the baseball diamond to discuss the philosophy of ministry within the Bethel nomenclature.

The goal in baseball is to amass as many runs as possible within the time allotted (in nine innings, with three outs apiece for each team). Each player on the field becomes a potential run when they come up to bat. Each player tries to get on first base, most often with the assistance of their teammates. The ultimate is to touch all three bases and come around to score at fourth base, identified as home plate or simply "Home!"

Titus 2:11-15 brings into focus the scope and sequence of the originator of our existence and His prescribed activities consistent in any individual's quest for the purpose and fulfillment of life. I believe that this scripture offers a tremendous foundation for any initiative premised upon intimacy with God. In addition, it challenges us to seek it, not only in terms of a stated goal and ideal, but also as a measurable reality in its real-time impact on the standing and quality of our lives in the here and now.

The next four chapters will present the four stages we have Biblically determined as essential here at Bethel Gospel Assembly. As a loving, learning and launching church, there is great emphasis placed on a team approach towards advancing each participant through various requisite stages, ultimately to be found "Safe at Home" in their eternal destiny.

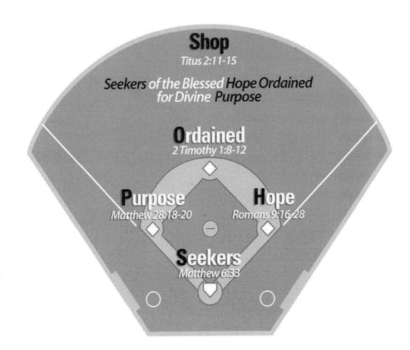

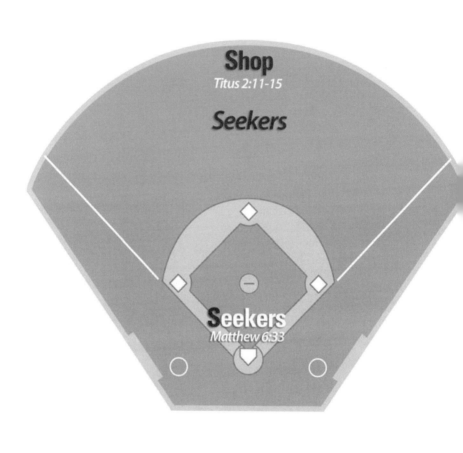

Shop
Titus 2:11-15

Seekers

Seekers
Matthew 6:33

6. SEEKERS:
NEVER TOO LOW FOR HIS HAND TO BRING YOU UP!

TITUS 2:11–12 says—

(11) *For the Grace of God that bringeth salvation hath appeared to all men,*

(12) *Teaching us that, denying ungodliness and worldly lusts, we should live soberly righteously, and godly, in this present world.*

Having been blessed to attend a Christian high school, New York Christian Academy in Brooklyn, New York, at graduation all of us students were required to include our favorite scripture for the year book. By seventeen, after having attended Sunday School since I was a toddler, I had learned the significance of many scriptures. To me, the one that seemed a best summation of an individual's personal goal in life is wrapped up in Matthew 6:33, which reads: "Seek ye first the kingdom of God and his righteousness, and all these things shall be added unto you." To me, this single verse establishes a sense of purpose, an effective means for crisis management, problem solving, course correction and a reality check. It gave me reason to get up in the morning, to hear someone say, "It will be all right" and believe it; to simply try, try and try again. Christ means all of that and much more to me!

TITUS 2:11–13 says—

(11) *For the grace of God that bringeth salvation hath appeared to all men,*

(12) Teaching us that, denying ungodliness and worldly lusts, we should live soberly righteously, and godly, in this present world;
(13) Looking for that blessed hope, and the glorious appearing of the great God and our Savior Jesus Christ.

For the reader today, this text addresses the reality of a world driven by a self-centered and overwhelming passion for self-gratification. It speaks to the sole means that make it possible to write a new script for our lives. This script leads us into the promises of a God not willing that any should perish, but that all should conquer the power of sin through living a life of repentance and obedience.

Whether through political, sexual, or material pursuits, the very fabric of our society has been altered from its original design, giving impetus to activities that feed upon greed and corruption, ultimately leading us to our deaths. It must also be emphasized that in this present society, liberalism is in fact the leaven and means by which this corruption and exploitation has taken place. But there are individuals emerging from the stormy gale who have acknowledged the hope that can be realized through seeking a committed life in God through Jesus Christ.

These believers give expression to the spirit-man within, which reminds them that there is more to life than the hard sell campaigning of the self-interested groups, tyrannical authorities and sexually addictive spirits pervading the social and entertainment playing fields of our society. These believers recognize a higher authority capable of "rebooting" their "hard drive", and initializing a process for divine purpose and destiny. The question for many is, *Where do I go to find it?*

During a recent crusade in Chicago, a young woman responded to my message of God's power to get the job done in our lives by sharing her testimony. As a young woman her life had been devastated; she had become a gang banger and a prostitute. Yet in the midst of her confusion, she remembered how God fought hard to rescue her soul.

She told me that one day she nearly drowned in a pool of water. Swimming alone, she foolishly ventured out to the deep end of the pool, finding herself unable to get back to safety. She sunk to the bottom of the pool before she had the presence of mind to call out to God. "Just then," she told me, "I saw this huge, glowing hand reaching towards me on the bottom of the pool, pulling me up to the water line, and then firmly pushing me to the shallow end of the pool where I was able to pull myself to safety."

She went on to say, "Years later, in the midst of my madness, I remembered what God had done for me then. I realized that my life must count for something for Him to have saved me in my recklessness at that time, and I believed He could do it for me now in my present circumstances. Calling on Him once more, I threw away my guns, denounced my lifestyle and chose to follow Christ. I am now living a changed life through the grace of God. I am learning to love and continue to seek Him daily, because He first loved me."

Unfortunately, the greater challenge for this particular seeker over the years has been finding acceptance in a church community that knows the facts of her past. Far too often the embrace of the Body of Christ has not measured up to what scripture led her to expect from those claiming to be the hands of Christ. In that sense it is essential that we remember that in the Christ-centered scheme of things, the seekers are sought and secured by churches that are aware of the issues that matter to the King of the Kingdom. What matters to our Lord is the saving and preserving of the souls of men and woman, not their past condition.

Today we rejoice to know that her present church has embraced her and others like her. Her pastor is a firm believer in the scriptures that state, "All have sinned and come short of the glory of God," (Romans 3:23) and identifies our righteousness as "filthy rags" (Isaiah 64:6). When we remember how far the Lord has brought each of us, we are more helpful to one another on our journey home.

The term "Seeker Sensitive" has become a buzz word in our

Christian circles. It has become an established concept in advising believers not to become so caught up doing our church thing that we forget that God's thing is to be concerned about the "uninitiated", those that do not have a clue what *our* Christ thing is all about.

Between my seminary class on church planting and Rick Warren's teachings on the subject through his book, *The Purpose Driven Church,* I became aware of this particular phraseology in the late Nineties. Prior to that time, as part of a mission-minded church, the need to present a gospel that was accessible to those who were different, or removed from our familiar ground, was inclusive in our approach to worship. The truth is Bethel Gospel Assembly, under the direction of Bishop Ezra N. Williams, had already established a sufficient, working evangelistic philosophy before the rubric of church growth became a fad.

Our teachings at Bethel made us conscious of the dangers of trying to "own" Christ and to corner the market on the "proper" spiritual expressions. We had been taught long before to be careful not to flesh out our spiritual experience in such a way that it would result in our failure to relate to the felt needs of others.

Of course, anytime you raise an interesting angle or idea, the naysayer will move in quickly to suggest the shortcomings of that inspiration. Much has been written about the simplicity of Pastor Warren's presentation of the "Seeker Sensitive" model, stating that "there is not enough depth," or "too great a measure of compromise on certain core values of our faith."

Any move that champions the Lordship of Jesus Christ and carries that truth beyond the four walls of the church is a step in the right direction. What I am wary of is any move that diminishes the active role of the Holy Spirit in the process. It is incumbent upon all spiritual leaders to keep their egos in check and be obedient to the *now* of God. We must always ask the questions, *What is He doing right now, in this situation, under these conditions? And What is the Biblical principle being enjoined; and how and by whom does He want the assignment carried out?*

I am reminded of a story about one family's peculiar culinary practice. During the preparation of a particular dinner meat, all the sisters in the family were trained to cut off the end of the meat before placing it in the pot. The day came when one of the sisters finally asked her mother why she always had them cut the meat in this way. Was there something wrong with that portion of the meat that was cut off? The only answer that her mother could give was, "That's the way my mother did it, and her mother before her!" Troubled by her mother's inability to give a satisfactory answer, she asked her grandmother the same thing. "You better call up your great grandmother in the nursing home and ask her," was her reply. When the old and venerable matriarch was finally asked why she always severed the end piece of the meat before cooking, she gave a very short and simple response—"It was too big for my pot!"

Harlem is populated with a number of small storefront churches that have remained static, in the same place physically and spiritually for decades. Some of these churches have remained the same because they have become family churches, meaning one has to be related by blood or marriage to take part in them. Others demand that you come from the same island or region. Still others have attached themselves to a particular practice or interpretation of scripture that has become so peculiar and obscure that even the mothers of the church cannot tell you how it started. Even though they are ignorant of the relevant function of their particular practice or interpretation, they are determined to defend its existence to the death, and so they shall, even to the end of that particular church.

Having traveled the world over as an observer of life and a lover of people of all walks of life, I do not have to rely on my college or seminary experiences to confirm the "seeker" element that lives within us all. In our quest for purpose, affirmation and satisfaction, we have been willing to go to almost any length to secure it. The twists and turns of our lives reveal our thirst for the thrilling and our hunger for a thunderous experience that will satisfy our mortal flesh. Whether we are born among the advantaged or disadvantaged, the god of this world, Satan, skillfully appeals to the sin nature in each of us. He does so to permanently derail us in our quest for and fulfillment of our divine destiny in Jesus Christ.

Even though we are encumbered with the self-defeating nature of Adam, thank God that He is the God of grace and mercy who has engineered our rescue. Luke 19:10 states, "For the Son of Man has come to seek and to save that which was lost." The naked truth of these words offer hope that we can be numbered among the *ecclesia*, or "called-out ones," meaning to become a part of the church, part of the Body of Christ.

In the true Body of Christ we have the truth seekers, those who respond to the gospel message of Jesus Christ our Lord. They are respondents to the truth of the revelation of God through Jesus Christ by a convicting and facilitating encounter with the Holy Ghost. In this experience we are built up into a correct and attractive relationship with Christ.

We are drawn to a Christ who loves us just as we are in the present. While our sins of the past condemn us, and our present circumstances make real the visible and invisible scars of our misdeeds and misfortunes, the gospel speaks of a God who says, "Come unto me all ye that labor and are heavy laden and I will give you rest." (Matthew 11:28–30).

Over the years I have had the opportunity to talk to thieves, murderers, drug addicts, prostitutes and more. I have heard how they arrived to that place of devastation in their lives. I have shared with many women who have experienced multiple rapes, beginning from their pre-teen years, and men who live in the shame of their own sexual abuse at the hands of a father or other relative, and have thus witnessed countless lives shattered by physical abuse, betrayal and abandonment.

Each of them have taken their place among those seeking an end to personal suffering; a place to find relief from their pain and to embrace a new beginning. What they come to know in Christ is that the Word of God is true. The arms of God seek to embrace any man, woman, or child willing to receive His love. It is our responsibility to get that message of hope out to the world. Far more than just words, it is our call to receive these individuals, these fellow seekers, into our own ranks where they can realize a new life within a nurturing, secure community of love and support.

Now that we have been brought up to the plate, let us proceed to first base. The next chapter explains just what that role of the spiritual community entails.

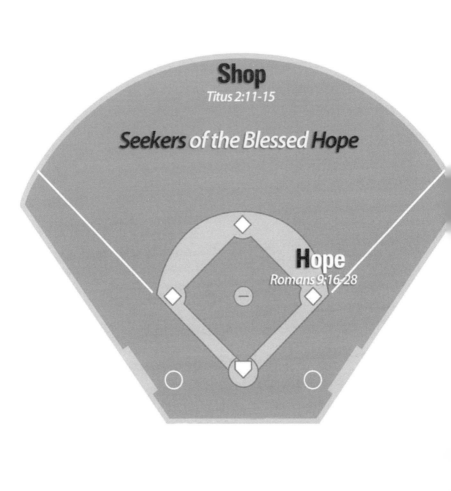

Shop
Titus 2:11-15

Seekers of the Blessed Hope

Hope
Romans 9:16-28

7. HOPE: YOU'VE GOT TO GET
THROUGH DINNER TO GET TO "FIRST!"

TITUS 2:13 says—

Looking for that blessed hope, and the glorious appearing of the great
God and our Savior Jesus Christ....

We ended the last chapter referring to one of the most critical elements essential to the establishment of a healthy and Spirit-led body of believers. This is the care we take to establish appropriate rules of inclusion governing the way new believers or transferring members are received into the fellowship.

For many years Bishop Williams shared a particular incident he witnessed on the island of Barbados that played a prominent role in his classic message, "Who's Going to Clean the Fish?" Unable to sleep late one night after a busy day of island ministry, he went for a walk on the beach and came upon some fishermen who had made a large catch that night. These fishermen were expected to replenish the supply of the many restaurants and homes on the island with a fresh catch for the morning market. Yet, early in the morning, though they had made a large catch, their feverish activity showed that their work was far from done. A new army of fresh laborers, with fish scales covering them from head to toe, were busily completing the work begun hours earlier. The fishermen's task would not be complete until someone had cleaned the fish!

Jesus identities His disciples as "fishers of men", which through the

51

above illustration beautifully demonstrates for us the divine expectation embodied within the process of fish cleaning. Indeed, it is this very function of cleaning fish that God would have us to elevate the day-to-day experience of the church to a science. Just as fish come in all kinds of sizes and shapes and different colors and varying conditions, so too are the souls that enter the spiritual nets that we cast into this sea called life very different. Each church should be organized to give the special care and nurturing our new arrivals need as we help bring them to the place where they can assume a responsible role in the service of the Lord.

Titus 2:14 outlines for us Christ's purpose and expectation through his death, burial and resurrection. "Who gave Himself for us that he might redeem us from all iniquity, and purify unto Himself a peculiar people zealous of good works." This scripture speaks of the transforming of lives through their intimate relationship with Christ to form a loving community of individuals with the same look and passion. It is by Christ's design that, through our zeal to demonstrate our love for Him, we faithfully project the glory of God through Christ-centered corporate action. The key word here is "love," which is another way of saying "Christ in action!"

At Bethel we constantly remind our people that we are not about religion, but relationship. Far more than our traditions, the beauty of our sanctuary, the liturgy of our services—over and above our corporate taste in worship music and style, it is the relationship we establish with our Lord and model through our *bridge relationships* with others that matters the most in the end.

In Luke 14, Jesus once again challenges His detractors and accusers on the subject of the Sabbath. Knowing that He was being set up (the man with dropsy was not there by chance), Jesus responds to the questions in their eyes (Verse 1 states, "They watched him"), revealing the state of their hearts and turns the table on them by asking them their own question, "Is it lawful to heal on the Sabbath?" Sensing a trap, they remained silent, and Jesus proceeded to illustrate the common sense of God that we often cloak with the traditions and vain interpretations of men. After taking the man and healing him, in Verse 5 Jesus inquires of them, "Which of you shall have an ass or an ox fallen into a pit, and will not straight way pull him out on the Sabbath day?" Again, they were unable to answer Him owing to the stubbornness of their own hearts.

After this Jesus begins to share important insights about the nature of God, His loving and giving character and His quest for relationship; the kind of deep relationship that is so intimate in its depth of quality that its impact leads to the kind of reflection that produces change!

I brought out some of these insights in a message entitled "Guess Who's Coming to Dinner?" This is one of my favorite messages, not just because of how it was received and impacted others, but because it brought a greater appreciation to my own understanding of God's grace. The message examined the question found in the text, "What is the purpose of the Sabbath?" In the text He challenged those who claimed to be the masters of religion and experts on the mind of God. In their dialogue, Jesus deftly challenges them about their true understanding of divine will and intentions.

Even as the spirit of the Sabbath is preserved in our worship on the first day of the week (as did the early church), my question is, "What is our purpose in being there as part of the body of Christ? How does our relationship with God—(worship, reading and listening as we watch Him) translate itself in our everyday life? Should it not affect change in the partaker—and produce an impact upon community?"

This message is brought out through two parables: a warning and a final truth regarding the value of salt! The first parable found in Luke 14:7–14 speaks to the humility with which one should approach those things that are lofty and high. Rather than operate on assumption, one should move in humility, showing that you have both studied and given honor to the Host who has called you to dine. This view is supported by the aside presented in Verses 12–14. The nature of the proud and arrogant is to take the invitation offered them lightly, with no true gratitude and allegiance in their heart for their host. At the same time, it is the poor and the maimed, the lame and the blind who recognize and respect the great opportunity given them. They are the ones who extend full honor and deference to the host.

Then comes the parable of the great banquet in Verses 15–24, where those who had been invited, when told all was ready to receive them, and in spite of their commitment to attend, came up with the following excuses not to come: One had purchased land and had to go and see! Another had secured five teams of oxen to test drive! Finally, one man had a wife to go home and (I imagine) to enjoy!

The folly in the excuses are clear when you consider that no one buys land sight unseen, purchases a car they've never driven, nor marries a wife they don't know. Not only did the guests break a commitment, but they insulted the intelligence of their host. Yet in the parable, Christ outlines the very things that cause us to break Sabbath. In the parable each item has significance in our pursuit of life by way of—

Security

Productivity

Posterity

The land represents our attempts to secure our destiny through owning a piece of green earth we can call our own. For good reason they say, "It is better to own than to rent." Is this a bad thing? Of course not.

Then the five teams of oxen spoke to productivity in that the five oxen represent the extent to which this man could declare his independence and his ability to rise to the level of being a lender and not a borrower. Again, this is not a bad thing at all.

And then we have the wife, which addresses the notion of posterity, the potential for children and heirs to all that one has amassed in life. So what's the problem here? Are we not to pursue that which adds resources to our lives? The answer is yes, except when these pursuits conflict and contradict our prior commitment to the Lord. And then the order goes out to the servant: bring in the poor and the maimed, the lame and the blind, and bring them in because they will appreciate the invitation and the opportunity. Not only the near, but also those far off (meaning even the Gentiles) for there is much room (meaning grace) in the house (the Kingdom of God). These will also be sure to display the gratitude that comes when great gifts are bestowed.

Here is where Jesus shares a critical warning in Luke 14:25–33. Simply put: If you are not willing to take what is dearest to you, whether plans or people, and kiss it goodbye, you cannot be my disciple. In the King James Version, the word "hate," as found in the portion that reads, "If any man come to me, and hate not his father, and mother; and wife, and children, and brethren and sister, yea, and his own life also, cannot be my disciple…" means love less than. He tops it off in that final verse, saying, "So likewise, whoever does not forsake all that he has cannot be my disciple." (NKJV) Speaking this in terms of our placing God ahead of our pursuits of the things of the world.

In Verses 34 and 35, Jesus concludes: "Salt is excellent. But if the salt goes flat, it's useless, good for nothing. Are you listening to this? Really listening?" (*Message Bible*) The meaning here is, reflecting—listening in the sense of receiving and doing. In effect, to emerge with a true reflection of the One we have focused upon, our Lord, Jesus Christ. The standard definition for salt speaks to the preservation from corruption and the accentuation of flavor. This text defines for us the goal of the Sabbath—for our lives to be preserved and flavored as we come forth in the image of Christ. Through our trust in God we are able to live, "denying ourselves, taking up our cross and following," on a daily basis, believing that He supplies our needs. Yet it is as a community of believers that we come to the place of Christ-like reflection through His love, to demonstrate for the lost the hope that exists through a personal relationship with Christ.

Through our servanthood in Christ, we are no longer fixated on the quest for security, productivity and posterity and are free to reach out to those trapped in sin, the poor, the maimed, the lame, and the blind to let them know a great feast is prepared for them in Christ.

JOHN 1:10–12 says—

(10) *He was in the world, and the world was made by him, and the world knew him not.*

(11) *He came unto his own and his own received him not.*

(12) *But as many as received him, to them gave he power to become the sons of God, even to them that believe on his name:*

It is amazing what the power of love can do. When someone of exceptional character and gifts comes into our lives, shows us kindness and compassion, and even makes great sacrifices for us, the most common and natural response is to greet him with gratitude. Our deep affinity towards them begins to create a kind of mirror reflection within us of those qualities we most admire. We might begin to dress like them, walk like them, even think like them. In time others may go so far as to accuse us of losing our identity, by trying to be them!

Such a high level of enmeshment can become troubling. But when we talk about true intimacy with God, built on understanding and appreciation of His love and intention for us, there is an expectation that this relationship will grow to where a reflection of the Divine is achieved in our daily walk. Those who were summoned to the banquet in humility, especially those that had no idea that they could become a part of those festivities, recognized a quality in their host that created a deep sense of gratitude and openness in their hearts towards the one who "bade them come." The high level of openness created through this special relationship made them pliable for an "extreme makeover" in the image of their host. In the Hope Community there exists the same kind of passion for continued intimacy with the One who called us out of darkness. This passion is shared among the believers in a manner that acknowledges the love of God and the process of God in the creation of His likeness in us.

Again, TITUS 2:14 says—
Who gave himself for us that he might redeem us from all iniquity,
and purify unto himself a peculiar people zealous of good works.

This act of purification requires a process in our lives that is akin to the refining of silver. In this process the smelter must make sure the molten silver is brought to the exact temperature necessary to purge the impurities that may mar the finished product. In a familiar illustration, when asked how he knows when the silver is ready, the smelter responds, "When I can see my own image!"

In the building of the Hope Community, God uses everyday people on the road to change. He expects us to work together to build a community of seekers who will celebrate the love and endure the purging process to achieve and maintain the hope of a life lived in Christ. The Pharisees thought that this could only be achieved by following strict rules, standards and traditions. Unfortunately, too many of our churches have adapted this same approach with pastors and church leaders trying to literally whip their congregations into shape. Christ came to teach that this can only be achieved through a loving relationship.

A favorite quote of mine fits very nicely here: St. Augustine said, "Love God, then do as you please." If we love God enough to want to do what is pleasing in His sight, then we need never worry about our conduct, because things which will not please God, will not please us. If we lack love for God, all the rules in the world will not keep us true to Him. The law tells us what to do; love us gives the power to do it. One of my Seminary professors described a powerful lesson in life when he stated: "Rules without relationship will lead to rebellion; Relationship without rules will lead to chaos."

I recall an incident that I encountered while serving as a site supervisor at a junior high school in the city. Our unit consisted of eighteen classes and my district supervisor had instructed me to set up a general session for our entire unit in the auditorium. Once they were all gathered in the audi-

torium, he began his talk, but a teenager in one of our more difficult classes became disruptive. Before either I or her teacher could react, my supervisor decided that he was going to use her as an object lesson.

Big mistake! The student had a reputation for resenting authority
and could care less who was addressing her or what he could do about it. The
auditorium was quiet as the two of them squared off verbally. Before long
he ordered her from the auditorium and she belligerently replied, "Make
me!"

My supervisor, a mild-mannered, highly intelligent, well cultured
Jewish man of average height from the suburbs, was one of those people
who could wield a big stick, but actually had no idea how to use it effectively, especially when dealing with a short, tough, foul-mouthed, street bred,
hormonally-charged fourteen-year-old girl. After being challenged in front
of two hundred and fifty students and their teachers, he had no choice and
had to at least go through the motions of *making her*!

While he headed steadily towards her, she looked like a volcano
looking for the slightest excuse to erupt. Having met her parents, I had some
insight into how her upbringing gave vicious spirits the opportunity to drive
her into uncontrollable rages. By now I had repositioned myself where I
could get a good look into my supervisor's eyes. "Did he have this one?" I
asked myself as he prepared to take charge of the situation and turn it
around constructively. Or did he in fact want to find a merciful way out of a
confrontation that could turn bad quickly. Bad for him and bad for the two
hundred-fifty kids, some of whom would like nothing better than for it to
escalate into a full fledged riot. That look in his eyes answered my question.
Realizing she was not about to back down, he had no clue what to do once
he reached her!

Grasping the situation, I got between them before he had a chance
to close in. Standing between the two of them, I quietly told her, "Young
lady, go upstairs to my office." Without a word, she obeyed my command
and spun on her heel and left the auditorium. With a quick, grateful glance

to me, my supervisor returned to the stage and picked up his speech where he left off without mentioning the disaster that had just narrowly been avoided. Rules without relationship lead to rebellion!

Her fist had been clenched and she was more than ready to pour out her fury on my supervisor. What she was not prepared to do was directly oppose or disrespect me or my authority. The reason was obvious. Over the previous few months I had been able to win her respect and confidence through simple acts of kindness and by maintaining a consistent presence in her life.

She knew I believed in her ability to achieve and would continue to support her in her pursuit for success. By revealing to her a God-glorifying love, her hope to do better had been revived. It was on the basis of that kind of relationship that even in the middle of her pain, she submitted to the rules.

The masks we wear make it difficult for people to understand the pain that we have endured throughout our lives. We come to the church seeking the better way and strive to make progress. As we grow together, sooner or later our masks will slip and our fellow believers will begin to learn our pain, despite our best efforts to keep them at bay. It is only in a supportive community that grows and shares that we can begin to trust enough to allow others to enter into the depth of our hurts.

In a Hope Community, the love of God displays the healing hands of wounded healers. We are referring to the hands that have begun the process of cleaning the calluses that have formed from the hardships of life, bringing us to a place where we can appreciate the body of Christ. It is through the affirmation of he men, women and youth who share our experiences with Godly support, sometimes gently and still other times with loving firmness, that we are led to spiritual, emotional and social health.

The Hope Community (those that agree on and commit to seeking of the blessed hope) is represented by the assembling of the membership into care-giving, mutually supporting vehicles for the purpose of *Followship* and *Fellowship*. At Bethel we are organized into various groups that allow us to link up with fellow believers with similar strengths and characteristics to celebrate our uniqueness. These groups include:

> Men-'N-Ministry (Men's Group)
> Alabaster Women of Faith (Women's Group)
> Youth Ministries (Imagine Center, NET.COM, Lion's Whelp Associates)
> Member Services (General Assistance to all Members)
> Family Ministries Fellowship (Married Couples)
> Sunday School (for all ages)
> Deacon's Support (for all members)
> Mission Prayer Groups (Groups for all members organized around prayer issues in the area of Missions)

Under the guidance of mature lay leaders, these smaller group settings offer many opportunities for healthy relationships to form, while at the same time giving individuals ample chances to learn the rules! Again, Bethel recognizes that relationships without rules lead to rebellion!

Having worked with youth for many years, I have seen the negative impact on families when parents raise their children without a strong understanding of the parameters that should exist in a proper parent-child relationship. How often I have heard the lament of parents whose children have lost their way because of their lack of respect for their parents because of the permissive way they were raised. Such children become a public embarrassment to the very parents they claim to love, and remain out of control in their family and social relationships today because they were never held accountable to the rules.

The truth is, God sets the agenda for the church and this agenda is to be passed down through the Pastor in the spiritual house. While Sunday morning preaching offers an opportunity to establish the vision and mission of the church, it is necessary for an alternative setting to be established for that Vision to be both rehearsed and reinforced. The Bible states that "iron sharpens iron" and it is through positive association within the community that maintenance and reinforcement of the Christ-centered Vision and Mission can be achieved.

As stated in the introduction to this section, Bethel's affirmation speaks to the idea of accountability, correction and transformation. It is understood that each church needs to be accountable in order to thoroughly tend to the spiritual needs of the flock. Two basic groups common in many churches include the work of the deacons (as members are assigned to each for crisis or for check-up purposes) and/or the Sunday school classes, especially when the church is structured to offer classes for all ages. Bethel utilizes both, but due to the size of the congregation there is need for improvement, as some individuals have been known to slip through the cracks.

We will talk more about the Sunday school in the next chapter when the focus is on the Christian education ministry. The role of the deacon is critical to the health of the church. The early church described in the Book of Acts outlines for us the genesis of this church office. In Paul's writings in I Timothy 3:8–13, we are taught the standards for qualifying the men and women to hold this key position. We will not rehearse these qualifications, but do state that we subscribe to the value of choosing carefully, with prayer, those who will carry this weight of responsibility and authority in the church.

We recognize that some churches have evolved in a manner where overall governing authority is placed in the hands of deacons. Such systems are useful for establishing checks and balances within those specific organizations and to protect the congregation from "pastoral abuse." While in the history of Bethel our Deacon Board has never operated with such sweeping authority, their participation through the years has been of great significance, especially in the area of accountability.

In the Seventies, and especially during our initial growth spurt (mov-

ing from about seventy to two-hundred adults), the only active minister in
the congregation was our Senior Pastor, Ezra Williams. During that season
of change the deacons were given a wide berth of authority. Many could be
considered as being of the Phillip and Stephen types found in the Book of
Acts, responsible for handling the Word during the outdoor campaigns and
overseas ministries, as well as on some Sunday mornings.

By 1980, Pastor Williams adjusted leadership all the way around, to
what was then referred to as a "plurality of leadership." This was when our
current Associate Pastor Gordon Williams and I were among three men
added to Pastor Williams' ministry team to create the entity still known as
our Pastoral Board. From this point on, the goal of the Deacon Board has
been to develop relationships with the particular members of the congregation assigned to their list. Every member is assigned a deacon: our expectation being that the needs, the strengths and weaknesses, gifts and talents of
the members will be monitored and developed through the ranks of leadership, facilitating the spiritual growth of both the individual and the church in
general.

While this system worked well initially, as the church grew in size, so
did the member lists of the twenty-odd deacons that served over the next
several years. Our deacons, now with lists of members numbering from forty
to sixty apiece, representing over two services on a Sunday morning, needed
a scorecard to keep up with their charges. In addition, while most of the
membership were low maintenance, there were always those who wrestled
with chronic issues requiring far more support.

Even with several ministers, coupled with the small group support
system offered by Christian Education Ministry, we have concluded that our
accountability system is in need of reinforcement. To build a stronger support base, we hope to initiate a home cell program called PACE. The letters
in the title represent the critical objectives we hope to achieve during the
monthly meetings to be attended by the participants. PACE stands for:

Prayer
Accountability
Curriculum
Evangelism

Those that are interested in small group dynamics of the home cell variety can refer to the appendix at the end of the book which gives more detail to this ministry model.

The objective of PACE is to build a community of maturing believers who will answer the global call to mission. We seek to gather believers that live all over the city, offering them the opportunity to meet in off-site locations, inviting friends, loved ones and even mere acquaintances to non-threatening, informative gatherings that will acknowledge Jesus Christ as their Lord and Savior, and show how to build strong lives centered on that truth.

We used the phrase "non-threatening" to be sensitive to those who have developed an aversion to the church as a result of the numerous, highly publicized incidents of ministry abuse in our society. Whether we call it pastoral or ministry abuse, the truth is that there has been public documentation of abuses of all kinds perpetrated upon the innocent in our pews. Whether or not such abuse is increasing, or people have simply become more outspoken these days, the religious order has to answer to the charges of misconduct among pastors, leadership and entire congregations who have misrepresented the Gospel message. These abuses represent those spiritual communities that specialize more in horror than in Hope.

Much of my training in seminary focused in the area of pastoral counseling, providing me extensive training and understanding on the subjects of personality disorders, dysfunctional family systems, mental illness and various counseling approaches, as well as the inherent tricks, or should I say "trips" of the trade. These classes and my career in public education gave me appreciable insight into what makes a good man or woman go bad, especially when their greatest desire was to help, not hinder, others in their pursuit of personal and spiritual wellness.

Why would a pastor, a health care professional, or a law enforcement agent suddenly throw his or her career into the garbage for an inappropriate relationship that everyone else could see was doomed from the start? Was it stupidity? The devil? Hypnosis? Maybe you can say it was one or all of these, but not in the way you think. Not enough time and resources have been given to training spiritual leaders on the basic pitfalls encountered while sharing your time and spiritual heart with a person in crisis.

Avoidance can never be the answer; successful encounters with individuals who are as capable of becoming the victimizer as the victim can easily be attained. This is accomplished when the counselors, and that includes ministers, are properly trained and equipped to maintain appropriate relationships with those they seek to help.

As I have stated, I am a strong believer in accountability and believe that this extends to the pastor as well. Bethel operates under a system where the Senior Pastor is the Chairmen of the Church Board of Directors, as well as the *de facto* head of all committees and boards within the church. Our own accountably, or personal system of checks and balances, comes through both the Board of Directors and the regular weekly meetings held with the full time staff of elders (our Senior Ministers).

This is in addition to personal times of intimate prayer and sharing with two men who are very close to me and who challenge me in any and every area of my life. Then of course, most importantly, there is my open and caring relationship with Lorna, my precious wife for over thirty years.

Enough cannot be said about the achievement of excellence, especially when establishing a community looking for the blessed hope, pursued and verified through proper study and training. As we advance in the Hope Community, each of us must diligently "carry his beam" in the building up of the community of faith and the spreading of the Gospel of hope to every nation. The Bible instructs us to "Study to show ourselves approved unto

God, workman that needeth not to be ashamed, rightly dividing the word of truth." (II Timothy 2:15). This brings us to the second base in our ministry approach, the understanding of God's ideal for ordination.

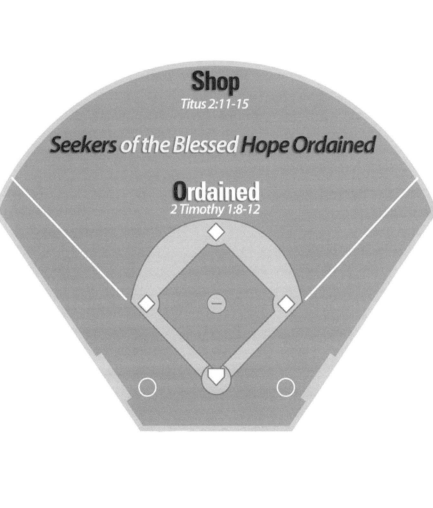

Shop
Titus 2:11-15

Seekers of the Blessed Hope Ordained

Ordained
2 Timothy 1:8-12

8. ORDAINED: "SECOND" IS FOR THOSE
WHO CAN FACE THE MUSIC!

TITUS 2:14 says—

*Who gave himself for us, that he might redeem us from all iniquity,
and purify unto himself a peculiar people, zealous of good works.*

News flash! God is not looking for fans in the stands! What He is looking for are those who will follow Him onto the field of battle. God is looking for those of us that will recognize through scripture that we have been ordained to serve His purposes and do not need a minister's collar to prove it.

One of the growing problems in America today is obesity. In response to a request from Congress, the National Institute of Health (NIH) released a report in 2004 that stated the rate of obesity in preschool children and adolescents has more than doubled in the past three decades, and the rate for children six to eleven years old has tripled. The report also said that approximately nine (9) million children over the age of six have now been classified obese. The report concludes that the amount of weight carried by the heaviest children is far greater than it was thirty years ago. In 2007 the Centers for Disease Control and Prevention reported that 34% of U.S. adults aged twenty and over are now classified as obese. More than one third of U.S. adults—over seventy-two million people—were obese in 2005– 2006 (33.3% males and 35.3% females).

One of the contributing elements to this epidemic is the proliferation of activities that relegate the masses to a spectator role. Too many hours are spent by the many watching the few "do their thing." Whether it is on the stage, movies, television, or a sporting event, we have become too comfortable living vicariously through the sweat of others, while our waistlines expand to unhealthy proportions.

This is also a reality of the church. Statistics from various surveys and study groups indicate that the church has created a *believer as spectator* reality. We have become guilty of consuming the worship and the Word, with too few being graduated to go on to actually doing the work. We may come out in record numbers in many cases. We have become expert connoisseurs of the best preachers and worship leaders. Our homes are filled with CDs and DVDs from the many conferences we have attended, while our bookshelves boast of the great expense we have incurred in the name of Christian education. Our computer hard drives contain our most cherished Bibles and Bible software. But eighty to ninety percent of the work of the church is still being performed by only ten to twenty percent of the membership.

More than ninety percent of our churches fail to promote the work of God through a viable missions agency within their own ranks. If successful marriages within the church are to be used as a barometer of the congregation's absorption and integration of Biblical truth in their lives, then it shows that we are hearers but not doers of the Word, as the divorce rate in the church is the same as American society at large.

God is not looking for fans, He is looking for followers! He says in Luke 6:46, "Why call me Lord, Lord, and do not the things I say?" In Mark 8:34 He says, "If any want to become my followers, let them deny themselves and take up their cross and follow me." Our *followship* is for the purpose of lifting up and glorifying the name of the Lord—to bear witness to this present and future generation—to tell them and show them who our God is and what He's all about. This presentation of the divine is communicated as a direct result of active participation in our Worship and Word study. As we anticipate the challenges that will come our way in this life, we must be prepared with a ready response, as I Peter 3:15 instructs, "But sanctify the Lord God in your hearts, and always be ready to give a defense to everyone who asks you a reason for the hope that is in you with meekness and fear."

Rather than live with the fickle spirit of a mere fan, we are led by the Spirit of God into a life of denial of self, into faithful connection with God in a manner that defies the temptations and trials of this life; with the intention to, through our spirit, present the true image of Christ to others. Matthew 5:16 says, "Let your light so shine before men, that they may see your good works and glorify your Father in heaven."

One advertiser talks of the "good hands people." God is looking for some good works people who can deliver the Good News that Jesus exists beyond the big budget Hollywood extravaganza! He exists through the dedicated lives of men, women and children who have responded to the knock on the door and let Him into their hearts.

Some years ago I heard the story of a Japanese aristocrat who was a great fan of the classics. In his desire to participate with the symphony orchestra, he used his great wealth and influence to buy a seat among the musicians in the orchestra, despite the fact that he had no musical training or talent. During the performances he would just sit among the musicians and act out his role. This arrangement worked out fine until a major change took place in the orchestra and a demanding and highly temperamental conductor was hired. He announced that each musician must play for him so that he could familiarize himself with their skill and determine their future role.

The moment of truth arrived, and it was now the aristocrat's turn to display his musical competence. The conductor ordered him to begin, but for several moments he just sat still, staring desperately at the music on the stand in front of him. After several minutes, he solemnly stood with his face bowed to the ground. His shame prevented him from making eye contact with the penetrating gaze of the conductor. When he asked what was wrong, all the imposter could say was, "I cannot face the music!"

It is guaranteed that everyone who claims Christ will face their moment of truth. There will be many opportunities and challenges for us to display the volume of truth we have stored in our consciousness and converted into conviction. Titus 2:14 states that He "gave himself for us, that he might redeem us from all iniquity, and purify unto himself a peculiar people, zealous of good works." Driven by conviction to commitment, we are presented as agents of God on the grand stage of the world, ordained to actively pursue spiritual warfare.

"To ordain" comes from the Latin, meaning "to put in order, to appoint."

> 1) To invest officially (as by the laying on of hands) with ministerial or priestly authority.
> 2) To establish or order by appointment, decree, or law is the universal definition that supports the concept of our election in God described in I Peter 2:9.

We have the formal definition of ordination that we use to describe the role of this critical area of leadership in the church. And then there is the general sense of the term, which speaks to the calling and the expectation God has placed in every believer as a temple of the Holy Spirit and an ambassador of His interests here on earth.

Referring back to the eighty/twenty distribution-of-labor syndrome in the church, I must emphasize that there is an over reliance on the "ordained" who are formerly recognized. It is expected that the clergy and their immediate support group accomplish the mission of the church and complete the expected level of study for ministerial proficiency. But there is not enough awareness that the purpose of God is fleshed out primarily through the Body of Christ operating in the spirit of unity, mutual accountability and the appropriate division of the Word of truth.

In the Gospel of John 3:5 and Ephesians 5:26, we recognize that the

70

proficiency of "performance" depends upon the degree of our immersion in the Spirit of God, and upon the cleansing action performed upon us through the washing of His Word. It is through the full acknowledgement of His love and will for us that we launch out towards the fulfillment of our purpose in life.

II Timothy 1:9 reminds us of this, as Paul invites his spiritual son Timothy to share with him in the divine enterprise through the power of God. Paul writes of the Lord as He "who has saved us and called us with a holy calling, not according to our works, but according to His own purpose and grace which was given us in Christ Jesus before time began."

As we have already signed up for the team, what is the process that equips us to face the music? There are no shortcuts, backdoors, or inside deals. It is through a personal commitment to excellence as taught by the Word of God! The Bible says, "Study to show thyself approved unto God, a workman that needeth not to be ashamed, rightly dividing the Word of Truth."(II Timothy 2:15)

It is essential that churches do more than focus on a Sunday morning showcase as part of a believer's spiritual routine. I am a firm believer that every child of God must take part in a systematic, Bible-absorbing process that will result in their personal and corporate spiritual growth. We must expose our congregants to opportunities for learning and experiencing spiritual and social building endeavors, knowing that He saved us to send us into a world of darkness that is in need of light!

The hustle and bustle of life in our urban centers is poorly suited to the dedicated study of the Word of God. By the following Sunday morning we find that we have been living off the fumes of the high octane truths we received from the previous Sunday message. The excellent Christian programming available in spiritual communities too often takes second place to the latest and hippest mind-numbing, soul-sucking sitcoms and "Movie of the Week" offerings that masquerade as quality programming in the new golden age of cable television.

Deuteronomy 6:4 represents the beginning of the most important phrase in the Jewish Book of the Law. It is the *Shema*, meaning, "To hear intelligently with the purpose of obedience," the essential creed of Judaism used to open every Jewish service and the first Scripture that every Jewish child commits to memory. "Hear, O Israel: The Lord our God, the Lord is one!" God = *Elohim*, a plural noun of unstated number that to my mind automatically defaults to the number three, which equals the Trinity! Jesus identified this Word as the first and greatest Commandment, the bottom line to the Ten Commandments and everything else.

MATTHEW 22:37–40 says—

(37) *Jesus said unto him, Thou shalt love the Lord thy God with all thy heart, and with all thy soul, and with all thy mind.*

(38) *This is the first and great commandment.*

(39) *And the second is like unto it, Thou shalt love thy neighbour as thyself.*

(40) *On these two commandments hang all the law and the prophets.*

(NLT)

This Scripture in Deuteronomy 6:4–7 speaks to the whole of man:

DEUTERONOMY 6:4–7

(4) *Hear, O Israel: The LORD our God is one LORD:*

(5) *And thou shalt love the LORD thy God with all thine heart, and with all thy soul, and with all thy might.*

(6) *And these words, which I command thee this day, shall be in thine heart:*

(7) *And thou shalt teach them diligently...*

Heart = Seat of mind and will.
Soul = Life and vitality.
Might = Strength.

These add up to a total presentation of emotions, thoughts and actions—learning how to love God through obedience and a committed lifestyle, wholly pleasing the Lord.

We are commanded to teach this discipline and disciple it through systematic training or subjection to authority; especially the training of the mental, moral and physical powers of the individual through instruction and exercise. The result of this training is that we establish the habit of obedience in the life of the one we disciple. To truly teach this lifestyle, we must submit ourselves to learn it! We can only learn it by experience! "It shall be in your heart!" You can only truly learn a thing through personal, hands-on interaction with that thing! The nature of that experience should be to the point that "It shall be in your heart!" (Deuteronomy 6:6)

Here at Bethel, we believe that an encounter with Jesus Christ can impact every phase of a man or woman's life. Such an impact is not made simply through spiritual promotion but by transformation that can be realized in physical healing, social acceptance and the realm of intellectual pursuit.

Fourteen years ago an attractive woman in her forties sat in my office and blurted out, "I need help!" Though we had never before met on a personal level, I was no stranger to her story. God had done a miraculous job in cleaning up her life. She spoke of a life filled with emotional, physical, sexual and even spiritual abuse. Her demon-filled, lust-driven life would have convinced even the staunchest believer to back off and pronounce her the hopeless victim of a reprobate mind. When others say "No!" Jesus says, "Yes!" One day the power of darkness was broken over her life, and with true repentance, she turned her life over to Christ. Praise God, now she could always be found in a familiar place in the pews, hands lifted in genuine praise and worship of her Lord and Savior Jesus Christ!

She came to me that day to share a problem that was nagging at her constantly. She could find no peace because of her sense of calling to do more for the Lord. She knew that she was saved to do more than just sit in church and occasionally give her testimony of deliverance. There was so much more in her heart to share and she knew her solution was in the pages of the Bible she carried into my office, but much of its truth remained locked away because she had never learned to read.

In our sophisticated nation—the land of opportunity—the truth is that her dilemma is a common one. This is especially true in large cities like New York, where it is common to find that a host of social, racial and economic factors have resulted in the "passing on" of a diluted, inferior education, leaving thousands of disadvantaged citizens ill-prepared to compete in the highly competitive job market. This woman faced great frustration. With her self-esteem increasing and with a new sense of purpose, what was she to do with herself?

Through the labors of the faithful and under the auspices of our Christian Education Program, a miracle gradually unfolded. Not only did she learn to read and express a depth of understanding and articulation of the Bible, but she went on to attend and graduate college, earning a Bachelor of Arts degree. She reached such a high level of excellence that when she retired from her job a few years ago she was honored by her employer, which had repeatedly promoted her because of her achievement and dedication. Today, she is a gifted speaker used by Almighty God at home and abroad, always careful to give the glory and praise to Him. God-glorifying transformation is always possible, and teaching is the element used by God to make it happen.

When God chooses to reach into His tool box and pull out an "instrument of righteousness" to get a particular job done, He does not want to use one that is dull or rusty. Those that hunger and thirst for righteousness, like this particular woman of God, are those that have a "use me,

Lord" spirit that drives them to study.

Some years ago the cry was "I want to be like Mike," referring to basketball great Michael Jordan. His great success is underscored by the fact that all you have to give is his first name and eight out of ten instantly know who you're talking about. Whether you are Mike, Lance or Serena, being great at what you do does that for you. This kind of hero awareness is played out in the church when we sit and measure the presentation of a man or woman to be of such excellent quality that we want to be like Pastor A or Brother B or Sister C. Why do we do this? Simply because they seem to have it so together!

What we believe is that each one of us can learn and grow, becoming the fulfillment of what we imagine in the lives of others. We can get there, not by being an observer but a participant in the process of transformation. We truly believe that knowledge is power, and so at Bethel we place great emphasis and care in creating an ever expanding educational program that meets the desire in every believer's heart to be like Jesus!

In the late Sixties, Bishop Williams began our New Converts/Members' Class. Originally six lessons, it now entails nine Foundation Lessons that help an individual to understand his conversion, basic elements of the faith, and the war that is constantly being waged between the flesh and the spirit. In these classes the individual student/prospective member comes to understand the purpose of the church, the purpose that he has now come to accept as part of God's plan for his life.

Each member is also encouraged to attend our Sunday School, the division of our Christian Education Department that has classes for students ranging in age from the "cradle to the grave." Even prior to purchasing our present location (which in fact is a former school building), Bethel always divided the classes up into different age groups, arranging each class to teach the Word of truth in an age-appropriate setting.

In the late Sixties, we added the Daily Vacation Bible School to the roster, and in the Seventies, Children's Church became an option for youth during Sunday services. In the late Eighties, Teen Church became a welcome addition for teenagers, as we kept our focus on the importance of investing in the spiritual and social education of our youth.

During the Eighties, we proposed to strengthen our Bible Study area at the church, and by 1990 we established the Bethel Bible College and Urban Mission Center, that teaches on the Bible Institute level. In time we also established a relationship with Oral Roberts University. While enrollment has yet to achieve the high levels we continue to work towards, we are constantly moving in the right direction by encouraging more of our community to become engaged in deeper study of God's Word.

Towards this end, several short term congregation and community wide studies have been offered through our Christian Education Ministry. The well known Southern Baptist discipleship curriculum, *Master Life,* has become a staple here at Bethel. Its presentation has been adapted by the highly gifted Reverend Joyce Eady, our current Minister of Christian Education, to reflect the needs of our community. We have found it to be a powerful tool for creating both an enhanced understanding and a better execution of personal devotions, and the establishment of a positive, God-glorifying lifestyle in the walk of the believer. Hundreds of our own members, as well as many believers from other churches and denominations, have taken this popular small-group, seven-month-program in the few short years since it was successfully initiated.

Along with these staple classes comes an array of study groups that come under the title, The Dominion Series of Spiritual Development for Men and Women. These learning opportunities include diverse subjects, such as prayer, counseling, sexual purity, spiritual and physical fitness, diet training and a host of others. In addition, we have our Ministers in Training (MIT) classes for those who seek official placement in our ministerial leadership, and the Emerging Leaders Forum (ELF), a program designed to increase personal interaction between college age young adults and our pastoral leaders in order to impart vision and direction towards the personal fulfillment of their spiritual destiny.

On any night of the week, including Saturdays and Sundays, one will find a class of some kind taking place at Bethel. Believing that as a Learning Church, each person has to be improving—growing in the knowledge of truth—these classes are geared towards advancing believers towards excellence in order to maximize their impact upon their sphere of influence.

Having taken second, now we are heading for third!

Shop
Titus 2:11-15

Seekers of the Blessed Hope Ordained for Divine Purpose

Purpose
Matthew 28:18-20

9. PURPOSE: "THIRD" ANSWERS
THE QUESTION—*WHAT'S IN IT FOR YOU?*

TITUS 2:15 says—

These things speak, and exhort, and rebuke with all authority, Let not man despise thee.

"What's in it for you?" one of our team members was asked during a medical mission trip to Pedija in the mountains of Venezuela. We were a part of a team sponsored through the Urban Global Missions Alliance (UGMA), an organization founded by Bishop Williams out of Bethel Gospel Assembly for the purpose of creating partnerships among other churches for global evangelism. Having run out of an important medicine we'd brought, the team members pooled their own money in order to replenish the depleted stock at a local pharmacy. The owner of the pharmacy simply could not understand why a predominately African-American group was making such sacrifices in this remote region of his country.

The young man who answered the pharmacy's owner was a senior resident from Bethel's Men's Discipleship program named Edward. Just a few months earlier, his life had been in turmoil as he faced certain death. A victim of violence, drug abuse and family tragedy, this child of African-American and Puerto Rican parents arrived at the doors of the church one step ahead of oblivion. Not quite sure what he was getting into, Edward knew that if he did not allow an outside force to intervene and change the course of his life, there would be no escape from the downward spiral of his troubled life.

What he found through the Discipleship program was far more than just the hot shower, good food and clean shelter that he received at first. In addition to the necessities, Edward found a loving community of men. Many of their lives were in a similar state of crisis, but they had found common hope by accepting the promises of God according to scriptures. Welcomed into more than just a philosophy of ministry, he was brought into a community of faith that expressed love just as much as they talked about it.

Now, just a few months off of the mean streets of New York City, Edward found himself ministering to the spiritual and physical needs of the poor in Venezuela. He was the right man in the right place at the right time to answer to the question, "Why are you helping these people? What's in it for you?" His response was straight and simple: "Nothing except the joy that comes from demonstrating to someone else the love of Jesus Christ!"

It was Bishop Ezra Williams' goal as the founder and General Superintendent of UGMA to create this organization for the purpose of promoting mission development among churches seeking to expand their involvement in the Great Commission. Our objective continues to be tackling various projects as an alliance of churches, thereby strengthening the resolve of each partner church to commit their time and resources to the Great Commission. As the Chief Executive Officer, it was my privilege to develop the infrastructure and ministry strategies for this organization. This resulted in our becoming connected with Venezuela through a major missions conference held in Maracaibo in 2001.

The same year, Gordon Williams, my Associate Pastor and UGMA's Chief Operating Officer, organized and led medical mission teams in underserved areas in Maracaibo and the surrounding mountains. Under his leadership, various physicians, health care providers and non-medical volunteers from New York, Connecticut, Maryland, Pennsylvania, Aruba and Curacao came together for this great endeavor. With willing hands from varying backgrounds, they gave their time and resources, working long, exhausting hours to meet the medical and spiritual needs of several hundred men, women and children over an eight day period.

One may ask, what was a predominately African-American church doing in Venezuela? Our answer is: Why wouldn't we be in such nations as Venezuela, India, Azerbaijan and Albania, along with the many nations of Africa and the Caribbean? These are all places to which our ministry has carried the gospel of the Savior by His command! The Bible clearly outlines the objective of each believer in scripture. Matthew 28:18–20 states in a clear and direct manner, "Go ye therefore and teach all nations, baptizing them in the name of the Father, the Son and the Holy Ghost, teaching them to observe whatsoever things I have taught you, and lo I am with you even unto the end of the world."

Back in the late Seventies, Bishop Williams related an incident that took place while on a missions trip to South Africa. After speaking to a group of young people at a local school in the city of Phokeng, he was approached by a white American missionary. Although congratulating the Bishop for giving an excellent talk to the students, the missionary then had the audacity to challenge him, asking: "What gives you (as a Black man from Harlem) the right to preach here in Africa?" Surprised by this sudden turn in the conversation, Bishop recovered quickly, responding with great conviction of purpose: "The Great Commission as written in Matthew 28:18 states, 'Go ye into all the world and teach all nations,' and that command applies as much to me as it does to you, regardless of the color of my skin or my geographical location."

For years this has been the challenge to African-American churches working to realize their purpose and full potential in the faith. Unfortunately there has been a projection of an alternate agenda adopted for black leadership outlining activities that run counter to the universal truths of the world. Over time too much emphasis has been placed on local church activities as a measure of community expression. What is needed among churches of color are more ministries that are not relegated to the four walls of a church,

81

or directed merely to the skin color assembled within. What is needed is an obedience to the will of God and the leading of the Holy Spirit, with churches coming into compliance with the Acts 1:8 mandate: "And after the Holy Ghost is come upon you, you shall receive power and ye shall be witnesses in both Jerusalem and Judea, and in Samaria and unto the uttermost part of the earth."

Myles Monroe has become a leading statesman on the subject of purpose, and he speaks to this topic with great depth and accessibility of revelation in such books as, *The Pursuit of Purpose*. One of his great statements declares: "Except the purpose of a thing is understood, abuse is inevitable." In fairness, despite the long record of documented abuse that has occurred both among the clergy and in the pew, such acts are the exception rather than the rule. It is important to remember that the human vessels that God has chosen to use are "earthen" (II Corinthians, 4:7). While the spirit is willing the weakness of the flesh at times prevails when we fail to maintain our walk in Christ.

How many doorways leading to error have been opened because the church has failed to properly address Biblical mandates that define the management of its people and financial resources? This is especially true in the case of leadership's failure to establish the complete vision of God for each individual life. It is the responsibility of leaders to addresses each member' responsibility to actively demonstrate love and concern for the souls of men everywhere, not just those sitting at his dining room table or the pew next to him. You cannot walk in Christ just by placing a dollar in the Poor Box.

As previously stated, there is a great excitement in the Christian community for worship, leadership, and men's and women's conferences. Whether in Dallas, Los Angeles, or Tulsa, they come, Bible in hand, with new books and CDs in their bags to take home. We have record numbers of church goers that are being exposed to powerful preaching and teaching. Each of these powerful conferences feature powerful men and women of God who share day and night on subjects that promise to build the infrastructure of the church or show how to be men of integrity and women of virtue.

But when the subject of missions comes up, there is an air of mild interest in the pulpit and disinterest in the pews. We may applaud the faithful missionaries and their exploits when they come home to secure badly needed support. When the baskets are passed, we scurry to find a few extra dollars to keep hope alive on the frontlines. But we breathe a sigh of relief when the visiting missionary leaves until the next time. His absence allows us to get back to the issues that appear to be critical to our immediate success and happiness because they are closest to us.

A healthy church maintains itself in the holiness of God and the principles of faith before the eyes of its neighbors. It also faithfully and strategically engages in the spiritual, emotional, physical and social concerns beyond the borders of its local community. More than just sharing a philosophy that promises a better life, the entire world needs to witness a working model that inspires the average citizen to sign on for the life transforming experience of walking through life with Christ.

Bethel has defined itself as such a church. Hardly perfect by any stretch of the imagination, nevertheless we understand that our power lies not in our perfection but in our direction. In the working out of our "soul salvation in fear and trembling," (Philippians 2:12) to further our quest to be blameless, we direct our heart and purpose towards the teachings and principles found in the Bible. We recognize that the Great Commission is not a great suggestion, but a mandate and expectation from the Supreme Commander Himself. The example of Christ and the Word of God directs us to share whatever we have with others in the full and certain knowledge that our lives are not our own. Luke 9:24–25 states: "For whosoever will save his life shall lose it: but whosoever will lose his life for my sake, the same shall save it, for what is a man advantaged if he gain the whole world, and lose himself, or be cast away?"

Soon after Bishop Williams took his pulpit to the street in the late

Sixties he was beset with a heart-wrenching challenge. Many souls were responding, especially those that used to hang out on the corner of 124th and Lenox, right outside the liquor store. I remember from my youth how there would be well over a hundred men and women, most of them drunk, socializing on that wide street corner all day and deep into the night; hopeless and helpless in their quest to find life inside a bottle.

But one of our greatest success stories coming off that same corner is Naomi. Up to the time we met Naomi, her life was a haze of alcohol, sex and violence. High most of the time, Naomi was a true product of the streets. She had mastered the art of the con, surviving many a close call and a prison sentence by sheer wit. Even so, one could see she was heading for an early grave.

During one of our soul-winning excursions, she was brought back to the church by some of the saints who caught her attempting to commit suicide. Securing shelter and care for her for the night, Naomi was grateful enough to hang around the church, but not quite ready to submit to Christ as her sole answer to life's challenges. So hang around she did, for the next full year. On any given day, if the church was open, Naomi would be there. The problem was, most of the time she was as high as the proverbial kite. Many a Sunday she would interrupt the service to sing her favorite song, singing loud, slurred and off key, "Pass me not, oh gentle Savior, hear my humble cry, while on others Thou are calling, do not pass me by." She may not have been ready to surrender to God, but she was convinced He was her only hope.

Despite these disruptions, and some vandalism and violence she perpetrated on her reluctant and at times bewildered church family, the young Pastor Ezra would use each outburst as an opportunity to remind the people: "It is for the Naomis of the world that God has established His church, for all of us have sinned and come short of the glory of God." At times the Pastor has jokingly referred back to those days stating, "I wondered when the people would rise up and throw both Naomi and me out of the church." It never came to that, and through this valuable object lesson, the church began to grow in its awareness of purpose and more and more of the saints surrounded this troubled woman with the love of the Lord.

As we got to know Naomi, it became evident that there was a great measure of the Word of God already resident in her despite her difficulties, and what was needed was the watering of the precious seed through the faithful hands of the saints. These saints are those that stand as the Word of God in demonstration. When she realized the degree of love that the hundred or so members shared with her, she gave her heart to the Lord and gradually came to the place of complete deliverance from the vices that held her fast for more than twenty years.

Today, forty years later, Naomi is well known as the Reverend Doctor Naomi Wright, a well-regarded and well-traveled preacher and teacher of the Word of God who supports herself in ministry working as a substance counselor and health care worker. Naomi is just one of many examples of how the power of God can, not only save, but also transform a life that is hidden in Christ Jesus.

Bethel began to turn in the direction that God had called for under the leadership of Bishop Williams. She had already performed a few missions abroad on the island of Montserrat and Aruba, but when these young people came back from the field, they formed the nucleus of the new teams that hit the streets of Harlem with the same zeal for souls as they had had in the islands.

While many responded to the gospel message, there was a need for a house of healing where the special needs of new believers could be addressed. While some happily accepted referral to ministry facilities in various locations upstate and around the country, many others would not or could not accept such placement. Most of these returned to the streets never to be heard of again. This was a source of great pain and disappointment for our Pastor and the congregation. Something had to be done that would maximize our impact on the total needs of those that were caught in our spiritual nets.

In the late Seventies, our Pastor and the Missions Committee, headed by Ruth Onukwue, M.D., began to seek God's face for the appropriate strategy to meet the needs of these people dying in the streets for want of a local facility. While much of our support of missions at that time focused upon the support of ministry in places such as Haiti, St. Vincent, Aruba, South Africa, Zambia, Nigeria and India, we were equally committed to the needs of our own "Jerusalem and Judea." The suffering in the streets of Harlem had to be addressed as effectively as our successful missions abroad.

Those prayers were answered when we purchased the James Fenimore Cooper, Junior High School 120 building. As partial renovation began on the building, leadership made sure that much desired community ministries, like Beth Hark Counseling Center and discipleship housing and training facilities, were slated for development and operation as soon as the resources of the church would allow.

In the inauguration of the Beth Hark Counseling Center in 1985, and the Discipleship facility five years later, the dreams of a Pastor were realized. He had long witnessed the destruction of too many needy families while lacking the required facilities to assist them. Since then, more home mission ministry services to the community have been added:

- Discipleship Men's Program
- Soul Release Prison Ministry
- Community Outreach (Saturday Mornings)
- Bethel Christ Community (Youth) Center
- Computer Center
- Spanish Ministry
- Church Planting Initiatives; and much more.

In addition, Division of Youth Services will soon have a facility on the fourth floor dedicated to meeting the needs of youth in crisis. This 24/

program will work in tandem with our Christ Community Center activities that are open to young people from around the city, offering a safe haven for youth in need of advocacy and shelter from abusive conditions.

God's purpose is for His church to be involved in ministry both home and abroad, to go around the world to teach the gospel. In April 2000, the Lord asked me to hold what we called "Passport Sunday," when all our members were asked to get a passport in recognition of the Great Commission mandate for every church. As we prayed for God's divine purpose in our lives to be realized, we brought our passports to the church service to show our compliance to His request. Through Passport Sunday we established in the spiritual realm our ordination and preparedness to respond to the call of God in our individual lives, be it local or global ministry.

Overseas missions have played a major role in the growth of Bethel. The words of the Lord spoken to the Bishop early in his ministry, "Sow abroad and you will reap at home," have not only come to pass, but have provided living proof to the short term mission endeavors galvanizing the hearts and minds of believers, especially young people, towards a purpose-driven life.

In our pursuit of global ministries we have held conferences and crusades in such places as Trinidad, Barbados, Nigeria, Kenya, Cuba, Venezuela, South Africa, Zambia and many more. We have taken the entire choir to places such as Russia and Azerbaijan, where the gospel could not be preached, but where they did allow the singing of our "folk songs" to be heard and explained. It was a wonderful time of ministry.

In addition to our support for missions, we have sent out a few of our own people over the years as long-term missionaries. Churches have been planted in South Africa and St. Vincent through the support and efforts of membership from this Assembly. As we continue to seek God, we hope to send out entire families in the near future, families who will make a lifelong commitment to the work of reaching the lost with the gospel of Jesus Christ.

Over the years, ministry leaders from around the country and the world have commended us for the large missions pledges that we gather each year, especially considering the economic base of our membership. We have at times sent over $700,000.00 a year in total missions support. This figure stands against a membership ranging from a 1,000 to 1,200 adult members. We do thank God for what we have been able to accomplish through the faithfulness of His people. We continue to pray to the Lord of the Harvest that He will send more laborers to the field. At present we have only three of our members serving as missionaries in the field and we need to do more in this area.

One of the greatest obstacles to sending more missionaries overseas is that many of our members wrestle with substantial credit card and student loan debt. They want to go, but our long-standing policy is that our overseas missionaries must be free from debt. Towards this end, we offer Life Improvement classes through our Dominion Series that address the importance of sound and spiritually responsible money practices and "How To" classes on debt reduction and eradication. The Crown Series is another curriculum used by our Christian Education Ministry in the past that has proven to be beneficial towards this cause. In the Youth Ministry we have brought this truth to our young people before they repeat the sins, and the debts, of their parents.

It is of vital importance to us that a vision of a life in Christ is planted within everyone who becomes part of this ministry. Here at Bethel we have learned to avoid the "Hold the Fort" mentality. Instead we follow the leading of the Spirit into the world, and seek to make His praise glorious in all the earth.

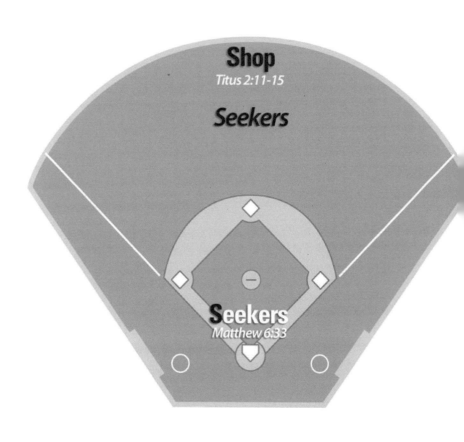

10. BRING IT "HOME": LETTING JESUS FIX IT FOR YOU
THE JESUS MODEL FOR SERVICE

At this point I shall discuss our overall approach to leadership. Leadership should never be left to trial and error, especially since we have the wonderful lessons given in the Bible of what God is looking for, specifically in the leadership model and example of Jesus Christ, our Lord and Savior.

Jesus models the heart and soul of a leader. He is revealed in the Old Testament script of Isaiah, Chapters 42–53, not only as the supreme leader, but also as a suffering, servant leader. What a wonderful figure of grace and mercy so eloquently displayed by the writer in Isaiah 53:4–12. This scripture provides a powerful message of hope and redemption that continues to this today as He is secured at the right hand of the father.

ISAIAH 53:4–12 says—

(4) *Surely he hath borne our griefs, and carried our sorrows: yet we did esteem him stricken, smitten of God, and afflicted.*

(5) *But he was wounded for our transgressions, he was bruised for our iniquities: the chastisement of our peace was upon him; and with his stripes we are healed.*

(6) *All we like sheep have gone astray; we have turned everyone to his own way; and the LORD hath laid on him the iniquity of us all.*

(7) *He was oppressed, and he was afflicted, yet he opened not his mouth: he is brought as a lamb to the slaughter, and as a sheep before her shearers is dumb, so he openeth not his mouth.*

(8) He was taken from prison and from judgment: and who shall declare his generation? For he was cut off out of the land of the living: for the transgression of my people was he stricken.

(9) And he made his grave with the wicked and with the rich in his death; because he had done no violence, neither was any deceit in his mouth.

(10) Yet it pleased the LORD to bruise him; he hath put him to grief: when thou shalt make his soul an offering for sin, he shall see his seed, he shall prolong his days, and the pleasure of the LORD shall prosper in his hand.

(11) He shall see of the travail of his soul, and shall be satisfied: by his knowledge shall my righteous servant justify many; for he shall bear their iniquities.

(12) Therefore will I divide him a portion with the great, and he shall divide the spoil with the strong; because he hath poured out his soul unto death: and he was numbered with the transgressors; and he bare the sin of many, and made intercession for the transgressors.

Our inspiration here is to be so in love with our Master that we go the distance to accomplish the mission required. We do so knowing that the greater work is already finished, the hard part done, and so whatever is required is attainable and sustained through the knowledge of what has already been afforded us through His sacrificial death.

Cyrus, the founder of the Persian Empire, had captured a prince and his family. When they came before him, the monarch asked the prisoner, "What will you give me if I release you?" "Half of my wealth," he replied. "And if I release your children?" "Everything I possess." "And if I release your wife?" "Your Majesty, I will give myself." Cyrus was so moved by his devotion that he freed them all. As they returned home, the prince said to his wife, "Wasn't Cyrus a handsome man!" With a look of deep love for her husband, she said to him, "I didn't notice. I could only keep my eyes on you—the one who was willing to give himself for me."

It is important for us to see that for His bride the Church, Christ paid the ultimate sacrifice. The response from Christ's bride should be equal to the response of the wife in the tale, with eyes and heart only for the one who was willing to give Himself for us. The church is to be so in love with and to become like "the Son of Man who came to give His life as a ransom for many." In the New Testament He speaks directly to the question of leadership as sampled in Matthew 20:25–28—

> (25) *But Jesus called them unto him, and said, 'Ye know that the princes of the gentiles exercise dominion over them, and they that are great exercise authority upon them.*
> (26) *But it shall not be so among you: but whosoever will be great among you, let him be your minister;*
> (27) *And whosoever will be chief among you, let him be your servant:*
> (28) *Even as the son of man came not to be ministered unto, but to minister, and to give his life a ransom for many.'*

Sacrificial "servant" leadership is at the heart of all that we strive to be at Bethel Gospel Assembly. It speaks to how we reach out to the lost, whether in our own community or across the globe. It also speaks to how we should treat one another within the Body of Christ. To fulfill our role as servants of God, we must understand that the acquisition of position in the Body is not for the purpose of lording over others, but for the purpose of seeing their growth and fulfillment as sons and daughters of God.

A wonderful example of servant leadership can be found in the life of my brother-in-law, Pastor Thomas Barclay. A highly educated man from a family of bishops, doctors, lawyers and educators, Thomas was an accomplished social worker when he was voted into the pastorate of Progressive Beulah Church on the south side of Chicago ten years ago. An exciting, humorous, at times unorthodox but always inspiring preacher, Thomas has brought a taste of new wine to a ministry that has served the Chicago community for over sixty years. Progressive Beulah was a sophisticated church, comfortable in its sense of duty to God. They maintained disciplined standards for what holiness represented and were fully prepared to give their full allegiance, respect and service to the man who was now slated to be the leader of the church.

From the beginning, Thomas pointed the church towards the hard streets which surrounded the ministry. The streets of the south side of Chicago were what you would expect in an area from which the wealthy have fled. What remained was a mixture of grand, well-preserved homes and businesses, settled in the middle of a maze of ruined, burned-out dens of iniquity harboring prostitution, drug-dealing, gambling, street gangs and death.

It was into these same mean streets that Pastor Thomas became known as "The Rev"—that crazy preacher "who comes up to us day and night and inquires about our health, our hurts, our hopes and dreams." He became their street pastor and never condemned them, but served them by settling their disputes, visiting their sick mothers, burying their friends, and hosting birthday parties for those who had never heard, "Happy Birthday to You" sung to them their entire life.

As time went on the church slowly began to see the vision and get with the program. Other members would join "the Rev" in his outreach activities that soon became a regular part of the church's program. Then they purchased the rundown building next door to house a special program for men. This ministry reached out to men that had come off of the streets and were well on their way to turning their lives around.

Soon the ladies of the church hosted a special gala for some of the female drug addicts and prostitutes beginning to frequent the church in search of hope and truth. They took them into the church and dressed them from head to toe in new underwear and decent clothes. Then they celebrated their lives as women that counted for something in the eyes of their

Creator.

It was not easy, and much of the struggle had to be faced alone by Thomas and his wife and family, leading the way by their example. In time this approach paid great dividends, particularly when he got an unexpected phone call late one Sunday night. "Hello, Barclay residence," Thomas answered. "How may I help you?"

"Pastor Barclay? Is that you?"

"Yes. Who's this please?"

"It's me! It's Leroy!" (Name changed.)

"Leroy! Where are you?"

"Your office!"

"My what?"

"Your office, Pastor! The door of the church was open and so I came in to call and let you know!"

Pastor Thomas was a sanctified believer in Jesus Christ, but he was not so heavenly-minded that he had no earthly sense. After calling a couple of the deacons, he dressed quickly and met them outside the church in fifteen minutes, bats in hand! When they went to the door, they found it standing wide open with the lights of the church burning bright. Expecting the worse, they found, much to their amazement, that nothing had been disturbed. A few minutes later Leroy came through the door with a few other members of his "street congregation."

"Hey Rev, it's me, Leroy." As it turned out, one of the deacon's had closed the church without locking the front door. During the night Leroy and a few of his companions passed the church, tried the door and discovered it was unlocked. At that point, a few of his crew began to emancipate the equipment and musical instruments that were now theirs for the taking. But as Leroy related to Pastor Barclay and his deacons, he told his boys: "We can't do that to Rev, not after all he has done for us in the street. We owe him too much!" Instead of running off with thousands of dollars worth of equipment to "cop a fix," they stood guard until they were able to reach the

Pastor. They did this because he had won their respect by serving them without judgment, despite their hard ways. This was their payment of respect to the kind of leadership that is putting a fresh face on a church that had lost its impact due to the abusive, arrogant and self-serving spirit that pervades much of the church leadership culture of today.

Today they cannot find enough chairs at Progressive Beulah to bring out in the church as the saved and unsaved come on Sunday mornings to hear from a preacher who did not come to be served, but to serve.

This concept of leadership has become a true challenge in our time. In many of our churches here in the United States, the idea of giving something for nothing has become a strained and strange ideal. The notion of doing service as "unto the Lord" has been challenged by a rising level of skepticism. As many churches grow in affluence and change their approach to ministry, this false spirit invading our hearts leads us to demand that the time and talent devoted to the poor be amply compensated by the trustees of the church. This mercenary approach does not bode well for the unfortunate who need our help to find Christ.

Now it is important that I say this, and I do so in all fairness. I lay some of the blame for this mercenary attitude at the feet of church leaders who have abused their authority and the treasury of the church to advance lifestyles that are inconsistent with the Word and the people they have been called to serve. I also acknowledge that part of the failure of some pastors comes as a result of years of abuse on the part of church boards who have failed to maintain adequate support for their pastors, as they try too hard not to "spoil" them.

Many families headed by faithful men and women of God have suffered from decisions made by church boards operating out of ignorance and meanness. As a result, some pastors, in their struggle for some measure of financial security, have been duped into embracing prosperity principles that represent a false interpretation of scripture, even though these concepts deny much of what Christ Himself represented and taught regarding giving and service. A new believer should never have to pay his way to Christ!

Today, many leaders have taken their newfound liberty to live in lavish comfort right inside their churches, even in church communities where the membership are hard-pressed to make ends meet. Many of these leaders have crossed the line into the realm of the mercenary; they are in constant search of "filthy lucre" as their reward for the pronouncement of divine truth or prophetic verse. Their example has given rise to the same cold and carnal spirit possessed by corporate America, a spirit that seeks only its own good and turns a blind eye to the plight of his brother.

It is important for us to remember that the Word tells us in Luke 6:38—

> *Give, and it will be given to you: good measure, pressed down, shaken together, and running over, will be given to you. For with the same measure you measure it will be measured back to you.*

Psalm 112 speaks to us of perpetual blessings that come from an enlightened opinion of those around us living under the yoke of poverty and oppression. The Word states in Verses 4–9:

> (4) *Unto the upright there ariseth light in the darkness he is gracious, and full of compassion, and righteous.*
> (5) *A good man sheweth favour, and lendeth: he will guide his affairs with discretion. Surely he shall not be moved for ever:*
> (6) *The righteous shall be in everlasting remembrance. He shall not be afraid of evil tidings: his heart is fixed, trusting in the LORD.*
> (7) *His heart is established, he shall not be afraid,*
> (8) *Until he see his desire upon his enemies.*
> (9) *He hath dispersed, he hath given to the poor; his righteousness endureth for ever; his horn shall be exalted with honour.*

Much of the breakthrough we are searching for in life comes from a willing heart and giving nature discovered in Christ. It is important that, as leaders, we establish opportunities for our people to come into the liberating reality of loving relationships that promote the good of others. This is the kind of spirit that only comes from studying the example found in Christ Himself.

A wonderful new friend of mine, Pastor Niyanka Manyika, has written a book titled, *Challenges of Leadership*. He makes the following statement about leadership:

> "Servant leaders are those who can express the nature of Christ the Lamb full of truth, and Christ the Lion full of grace....what kind of servant was He? Jesus served the people, ministered to them and put their interests first before His own. It is also clear, however, that He never gave Himself over to their will. According to John 2:23-25, when He was in Jerusalem at Passover during the day of the feast, many were converted and believed in His name as a result of the miracles that He did. He, however, "...did not commit Himself unto them, because He knew all men, and needed not that any should testify of man: for He knew what was in man."

Jesus understood that it was never the Father's intent to sentence leadership to the prison of the people's will. He was sensitive to their needs, responding to them when it was in His power to do so, as long as their demands did not divert Him from His call. To Jesus, servant leadership meant not only leadership by serving, but also serving by leading.

The latter is recognition that the leadership we provide is our service to God's people, even if it involves exercising the kind of authority people do not associate with a servant. While we may not naturally think of someone who exercises authority over us as a servant, Jesus describes His resolute and decisive leadership as servant leadership.

These types of leaders recognize not only their responsibility to do more than preach about service, but to also "model it" into the minds and hearts of the people they lead. Some of the greatest pleasure I find in church is when I have the opportunity to give direct service to our people. No, I mean beyond the counseling, or the teaching. I mean waiting on a table, or tying the shoelaces of a child, or helping someone to clean up the mess created while serving others. Many times when I attempt to help in these simple ways I get chased off by other well-meaning members. "No Pastor, let me do that!" And I let them, because the power of my example is working and it is important that they make this kind of service a part of their lives. Not only because others need their help, but because it is so healthy for their own soul.

This is another reason why I love going out into the mission field. Once there, everyone is too busy doing their own ministry to get in the way of my personal service to the people. But as Dr. Manyika points out, it is also so important that leaders do not allow their service to others get in the way of knowing what their ultimate mission is in the face of God. We are to serve while keeping the divine cause in plain sight, but we are also to serve because God has a master plan and a great standard that governs all we do. In doing your service to the Lord, in the words of Bishop Williams, never let anyone come across as "bigger than the cause."

I believe Bishop Ezra Williams lived that example when our church began to cater to the needs of the drunks, drug addicts and prostitutes that began to hang out at our church services in the late Sixties. Certainly they seemed to be out of place, especially at a holiness-oriented church like Bethel. "At the very least, sit them in the back where they will not be in the way of our worship," was the feeling of many in the church. But Bishop Williams held his ground at a time when it could have cost him the pastorate. Faithful to his calling, he argued through scripture that these were the very people that cost Jesus the support of the Pharisees and the religious leaders of his day. Who in the world would want to be categorized with them?

The way Bishop Williams held on to his position as a servant leader answerable to God as defined by scripture is directly linked to how our ministry is blessed today. The servant leader is one who allows Christ and the scriptures to define the scope of ministry for the membership, not the other way around. If this is to be the case, it is important that the membership correctly defines and assumes their role as leaders in the Body of Christ. They must approach this in a way that goes way beyond the mere possession of a title or an office in the church. They must commit themselves by offering their hands and gifts in a spirit that transcends the traditional or democratic process, but remains in accordance with the Word of God and the leading of the Holy Spirit. The next and final chapter will present us with an approach that servant leaders can follow to work together in community, and for the community to follow to fulfill the divine mandate for His church.

11. MEETING THE SEEKER!

For those who love a "how to do it" approach, here is a ministry model we have constructed as a guide for effective leadership. This model addresses the quality of leadership execution and membership performance we expect from those in our ministry. I simply call it the S.E.R.V.I.C.E Model and here is how it breaks down:

SECURE THE DIRECTION

EVALUATE THE RESOURCES

REACH THE TARGET

VERIFY THE MISSION: THE SERVICE BEING RENDERED

INTERPRET THE MESSAGE

COMMIT TO THE TARGET

EXPAND THE HORIZON

SECURE THE DIRECTION!

It is said that "if you don't aim at anything, you'll hit it every time." The clear defining of the direction insures that each leader understands the vision of the set man, the Senior Pastor of the church and the specific goals of the endeavor in which they have been called to serve. They must be clear about the core values and the mission of the church.

All that is done within the performance of their task must reflect this understanding, thus it is imperative that each individual leader fully understands the big picture. How does his assignment relate to the whole? What aspects of the vision is he or she being asked to undertake? What is the scope of the contribution they are being asked to make?

In the planning and performance of our mission there remains the constant threat that the challenges we face could cause us to lose sight of our purpose and how it fits into the grander scheme. Jesus had to address this very thing, and made it a point to enlighten and reconnect a man He considered one of the greatest men to ever live.

MATTHEW 11:1–11 says—

(1) *And it came to pass, when Jesus had made an end of commanding his twelve disciples, he departed thence to teach and to preach in their cities.*

(2) *Now when John had heard in the prison the works of Christ, he sent two of his disciples,*

(3) *And said unto him, Art thou he that should come, or do we look for another?*

(4) *Jesus answered and said unto them, Go and shew John again those things which ye do hear and see:*

(5) *The blind receive their sight, and the lame walk, the lepers are cleansed, and the deaf hear, the dead are raised up, and the poor have the gospel preached to them.*

(6) *And blessed is he, whosoever shall not be offended in me.*

(7) *And as they departed, Jesus began to say unto the multitudes concerning John, What went ye out into the wilderness to see? A reed shaken with the wind?*

(8) *But what went ye out for to see? A man clothed in soft raiment? behold, they that wear soft clothing are in kings' houses.*

(9) *But what went ye out for to see? A prophet? yea, I say unto you, and more than a prophet.*

(10) *For this is he, of whom it is written, Behold, I send my messenger before thy face, which shall prepare thy way before thee.*

(11) *Verily I say unto you, Among them that are born of women*

there hath not risen a greater than John the Baptist: notwithstanding
he that is least in the kingdom of heaven is greater than he.

Though described to be a great servant in God's economy, there came a point where John the Baptist was becoming concerned and perhaps discouraged because of the indignities and threats he had to endure while imprisoned by Herod. In his despair he was wondering why the Messiah was not making quick work of his enemies and ushering the Kingdom of God into place with all its splendor. But Jesus knew John's heart and its preparedness to acquiesce to the will of God. So through simply demonstrating the signs and wonders that were associated with the Messiah, he helped John the Baptist to remember his place and his calling. Through Jesus' action of healing the sick and ministering to the needs of those that were marginalized, He knew that John would regain recognition of the scope of the task, and intuitively understand his own role in the process. Without a doubt, when John the Baptist was eventually beheaded, he went to his death rejoicing in his heart that the Kingdom of God was indeed at hand!

I say to my leaders, "Don't write checks that I can't cover." It is important that my leaders are clear as to the purpose and the price of our undertaking. The purpose is the Glory of Christ, and the price is the gratitude and complete obedience we radiate through His grace and goodness. Every assignment must line up not only to the end result, which is the glory of God and the securing of souls; but also line up through means that are equally sanctified and God glorifying.

EVALUATE THE RESOURCES!

Assess the resources and supporting cast needed for quality presentation. Assume nothing—Check! Check! Check it again in a timely and agreeable fashion to make sure you have everything in place to carry out your assignment.

In speaking of duty and service, Luke 14:26-30 says, "No man goes to battle except they count the cost." This means that we will take special care to evaluate not only what the mission requires in the material sense, but also the measure of service required from a discipleship standpoint (Verse 27—"And whosoever doth not bear his cross, and come after me, cannot be my disciple.") Careful evaluation ensures that the effort will not be troubled by confusion or reflect poorly upon the name of Christ, but will show precision and a spirit of excellence.

LUKE 14:28–30 says—

(28) *For which of you, intending to build a tower, sitteth not down first, and counteth the cost, whether he have sufficient to finish it?*
(29) *Lest haply, after he hath laid the foundation, and is not able to finish it, all that behold it begin to mock him,*
(30) *Saying, This man began to build, and was not able to finish.*

The greatest resource in any task undertaken rests in the measure to which we abide in Christ.

JOHN 15:1–8 says—

(1) *I am the true vine, and my Father is the gardener.*
(2) *He cuts off every branch in me that bears no fruit, while every branch that does bear fruit he prunes so that it will be even more fruitful.*
(3) *You are already clean because of the word I have spoken to you.*
(4) *Remain in me, and I will remain in you. No branch can bear fruit by itself; it must remain in the vine. Neither can you bear fruit unless you remain in me.*
(5) *I am the vine; you are the branches. If a man remains in me and I in him, he will bear much fruit; apart from me you can do nothing.*
(6) *If anyone does not remain in me, he is like a branch that is thrown away and withers; such branches are picked up, thrown into*

the fire and burned.

(7) If you remain in me and my words remain in you, ask whatever
you wish, and it will be given you.

(8) This is to my Father's glory, that you bear much fruit, showing
yourselves to be my disciples. (NIV)

We are reminded by the text that Christ remains our greatest resource and means of achieving our purposes. This connection in Christ also provides the parameters in which we work, thus limiting our resources to those places, persons and things that uphold a Kingdom connection. How many times has Christian service attempted to advance the cause of God, but failed to do so through an operation soaked in prayer; launched with understanding that fully acknowledges Christ, with feet directed along the single path of His choosing?

Yes, Jesus paid it all, and to Him we owe all we have and do. We owe him our homework, our timely responses, our advance scouting and our budget analysis. We most of all owe Him anointed and faithful servitude, with hearts that are right and hands that are clean for His divine enterprise. Many a ministry or service for the Lord has failed to achieve its goal because of "the secret and presumptuous sins" of those involved, or due to the failure to make a proper study and accounting of the resources needed to accomplish the task. It is important that we know who we are laboring with, and to determine that we are on the same page in terms of what is at stake in our service to God.

REACH THE TARGET!

Reach, not breach, the connection with the target by an intentional, Christ-centered approach designed to meet the desired goal. We are to keep paramount in our minds that those we are called to serve must be ministered to through a God-ordained standard that speaks accurately of the person, and mission, of Christ. When serving the hungry, our kitchens must always serve two kinds of soup simultaneously. We must serve the soup that nourishes the body, but cannot fail to serve the other that nourishes the soul. It is clear that the Christ-centered connection we establish when serving others must not only take into account their felt needs, but must also extend to reach their real need, a viable relationship with their Lord and Savior Jesus Christ.

Their real need is to know the meaning and God-ordained expression of love! Not only must this be our guiding principle for committing resources to our projects, but it must also be the manner in which we execute our task. How we approach our assignment must be in harmony with the predetermined standards set for us in Christ. It is not just what we do, but also how we do it that counts. Our activities for the Kingdom of God are to be bathed in love, regulated by our abiding love relationship in Jesus Christ.

JOHN 15:9–17 says—

(9) *I have loved you even as the Father has loved me. Remain in my love.*

(10) *When you obey me, you remain in my love, just as I obey my Father and remain in his love.*

(11) *I have told you this so that you will be filled with my joy. Yes, your joy will overflow!*

(12) *I command you to love each other in the same way that I love you.*

(13) *And here is how to measure it—the greatest love is shown when people lay down their lives for their friends.*

(14) *You are my friends if you obey me.*

(15) *I no longer call you servants, because a master doesn't confide in his servants. Now you are my friends, since I have told you everything the Father told me.*

(16) *You didn't choose me. I chose you. I appointed you to go and produce fruit that will last, so that the Father will give you whatever you ask for, using my name.*

(17) *I command you to love each other.* (NLT)

The end results of lives that abide in Christ are depicted here as branches nourished by the vine. Our lives are not only sustained as healthy branches or extensions in Christ, but through the joy-producing reality of that attachment we come to the place where we produce the "fruit that remains!" The fruit reflects the quality of care and concern attached to our service. Christ also makes it clear in the text that He no longer calls us servants, prone to operate from an emotionally detached sense of obligation. Instead He calls us friends, trusted individuals whose attention to the details of our Christian assignments must equal or surpass the attention we invest in our own business.

A couple of years ago we had a play at our church, and the community response was unbelievable. The lines wrapped around the corner as hundreds came to see this challenging production depicting the reality of hell and the hope we have for salvation in Christ. On the last day of the play the lines were three times longer than they'd been all week long.

In the excitement, and in some cases, panic of dealing with so many people at once, some of our workers forgot the object of the evening and began to address some of the seekers in a manner that failed to maintain connection to those we were seeking to reach for the Lord. Most of the people that filled the sanctuary that night had never been inside a church before. While they did sit patiently in our overcrowded sanctuary, the auditorium sounded more like Madison Square Garden before a big game than a house of worship.

Forgetting the importance of reaching the target within the love of God, some of our volunteers began to be insensitive to some of our guests. In their zeal to preserve the dignity of our sanctuary they began to speak rudely to some of those seeking seats in the balcony, as they informed them there was no more room and they had to leave. The God connection we were seeking to establish was immediately breached.

With their feelings hurt, this particular group of about a dozen people headed for the exit as one of them, a young Latin woman, said loudly, "You see how they do you in church? I will never, ever go to a church again in my life!" Thank God my wife Lorna was going up the stairs to the balcony at that very moment. She intercepted the group, and while quickly introducing herself, made apologies for the church and for me personally. She took great pains to restore the God connection by assuring them that this was not what we wanted them to experience in the house of God. Showing love and humility she persuaded them to join a growing number of others guests hoping to see the production as we tried to make whatever accommodation possible to make room for them to view that powerful play.

By this time, over five hundred additional people had gathered around the church wanting to see the play. We had reached the masses, but now the success of the night had to be judged by how we maintained our God connection through our contingency planning. If they failed to see the love of God displayed by real people, not just actors on a stage, then the whole enterprise would be a failure regardless of the critical acclaim received by the production itself.

As it turned out, not only were we able to arrange for a double feature that night for the overflow crowds that showed up, but God allowed us to find seats at the first show for the original party that expressed its dissatisfaction with their initial treatment. The best part of it was that everyone in that party joined the large group that came forward at the end of the performance to give their hearts to the Lord!

It wasn't enough for us just to do the production. It was more important that we handled the production in a way that measured up to our original purpose: to introduce Christ to the lost. The target group was not the believers; those you could expect to know how to handle themselves in the house of God. This opportunity was being offered to a target group of unbelievers who did not have the proper training, but had the same need to see the spiritual play and surrender their lives to the love of Jesus Christ.

The people that came to our church that night might have come for a night of good entertainment (their felt need) but they came away with joy and a new lease on life (their real need—their love in Christ!).

VERIFY THE MISSION: THE SERVICE BEING RENDERED

Once we confirm our connection with the target group, be sure that the ensuing activities are consistent with the vision and desired outcome. Be prepared to make adjustments. This requires that we not only make connections, but evaluate the level to which these connections are accomplishing the goal.

Ongoing communication and accountability are the key ingredients here. Just as it "takes a village to raise a child", it is important that those asked to serve on the project operate with understanding and mutual respect in the allocation of resources and review of the plans. It is vital that we remain accountable to one another, making sure that we are hearing and following God's ordained course of action.

In Luke, Chapter 9, upon Jesus' return from the Mount Transfiguration, He corrected the course of action the disciples wanted to take, based on their well-meaning but misguided understanding of Christ's mission and purpose. First they argued over who was the greatest in the Kingdom of God.

LUKE 9:46–48 says—

(46) *Then there was an argument among them as to which of them would be the greatest.*

(47) *But Jesus knew their thoughts, so he brought a little child to his side.*

(48) *Then he said to them, "Anyone who welcomes a little child like this on my behalf welcomes me, and anyone who welcomes me welcomes my Father who sent me. Whoever is the least among you is the greatest."* (NLT)

It is necessary in all of our endeavors as Committee and Board members that we launch our initiatives after clearly establishing mutual submission within the group. We need to make it clear that "No BIG I and little u" attitudes need apply. The project leader should assess and allow for the contributions of each member serving the project. In our unity of the spirit we should be able to make allowances for the diversity of gifts represented in our ranks. We must take care to guard against the ego-flexing that tends to plague all of us at one time or another.

Whether it is out of insecurity, or due to a rough season that has moved into our personal lives, when we fail to submit to honest evaluation through the counsel of those speaking the truth in love, we can become dangerous to the cause. It is important that regular checks be maintained, not only on the progress of our assignment, but also on the spiritual health of those on our team. Then the disciples fussed because someone was following their program outside their group.

LUKE 9:49–50 says—

(49) *John said to Jesus, "Master, we saw someone using your name to cast out demons. We tried to stop him because he isn't in our group."*
(50) *But Jesus said, "Don't stop him! Anyone who is not against you is for you."* (NLT)

Don't you just hate the part of our nature that exhibits any tinge of jealousy, or delights in the failure of others? Never is this ugly truth more obvious than when "the others" are in the same business as yourself and are part of a "rival" group. Because they are not of our church organization, religious view, or race, we find ourselves saying, like the show biz people, "break a leg." Deep down inside the truth is we are ashamed to admit we meant it literally!

How we react to others during the course of our service not only sends an indication to the other group about your spiritual depth, but also imparts a loud message to those we have been called to serve. It is not so much what they hear from us that impacts those we are reaching out to with the gospel, but what they see in us that has the final word!

Finally, they were prepared to display the wrath of God because some folk were not inclined to receive their message.

LUKE 9:51–56 says—

(51) *As the time drew near for his return to heaven, Jesus resolutely set out for Jerusalem.*

(52) *He sent messengers ahead to a Samaritan village to prepare for his arrival.*

(53) *But they were turned away. The people of the village refused to have anything to do with Jesus because he had resolved to go to Jerusalem.*

(54) *When James and John heard about it, they said to Jesus, "Lord, should we order down fire from heaven to burn them up?"*

(55) *But Jesus turned and rebuked them.*

(56) *So they went on to another village.* (NLT)

How many times were you ready to give up on someone or something because of their opposition to your ministry or gesture of kindness? Then you think, "You had your chance, so now you can just go to…" Oh no! Is that Christ speaking through you, or is it your own expression of frustration that has taken over the mission? All of us are prone to this kind of temptation from time to time, but it is only in an authentically healthy accountable Christian relationship that we are able to guard ourselves to avoid betraying the mission we have been entrusted with.

During a recent mission, I had, in my mind at least, ample reason to wipe the dust from off my shoes and write, "Ichabod" over those that failed to live up to their promises. But through prayer and counsel I came to understand God's greater purpose beyond my disappointment and frustration. As a result, a greater work than I could ever have imagined had been erected to promote the name of the Lord. This brings us neatly to our next point.

INTERPRET THE MESSAGE!

What is the message you hope to send through your activity or service? Does it speak well of the faith you pledge, or does it accomplish only a physical goal, bereft of a true demonstration of the nature and mission of Christ? When the task is done, have you raised the awareness and understanding of your target group into a correct and balanced interpretation of Christ (His person), the Bible (His Word), and the Church (His reflection, the Body of Christ)?

Long before President Bush became faith-based friendly, Bethel Gospel Assembly was offering goods and services to the community, the lion's share of the support coming from members of the church. Since that time, opportunities have come that allowed us to become fully funded for services such as our food program. The plain truth about some of this support is that it came with strings attached.

Each week, hundreds of individuals join us in our Fellowship Hall for healthy meals prepared by our team working out of our Beth Hark Crisis Counseling ministry. While enjoying their meals, we spend time sharing with them the love of Christ and the services we offer to help them meet their spiritual and social challenges. According to government agency rules, we would not be allowed to do this if we were to receive their program funding.

As much as we need their help financially, we can never lose sight of our mission, nor compromise the message we want to send. The message is that Jesus is able to meet the whole needs of man. There may be ways of working around the red tape, but Bethel Gospel Assembly will always operate our ministry by applying the most exacting standards of Christian ethic that will never shame us before the people of God or the laws of the land.

112

Our large facility contains two gyms, a fellowship hall, classrooms, meeting rooms, etc. It would be easy for us to get caught up in basketball leagues, hosting community action meetings, cooking clubs and the like, while failing to maintain the spiritual connections and values that must be associated with all such endeavors. While we encourage the youth of our community to come use our gym, we make sure that somewhere within the programs, in concrete, discernable ways, they learn the name and the nature of their true host, Jesus Christ our Lord. Whatever creative and seeker-friendly approach we use to meet the masses, it is important that they are able to take away more knowledge and truth about the love of God through our Savior, Jesus Christ and His Church, than they came to us with.

COMMIT TO THE TARGET!

Plan for, and be prepared to go the extra mile to bring God glorifying closure to your assigned phase of the task. Be prepared for contingency planning and even more prepared to spend yourself!

In MATTHEW 16:24–26, Jesus said—

(24) Then Jesus said to the disciples, If any of you wants to be my follower, you must put aside your selfish ambition, shoulder your cross, and follow me.

(25) If you try to keep your life for yourself, you will lose it. But if you give up your life for me, you will find true life.

(26) And how do you benefit if you gain the whole world but lose your own soul in the process? Is anything worth more than your soul?

have found my wife Lorna to be an excellent example of this component of the S.E.R.V.I.C.E. Model. As a loving wife and caring mother of our children, she has made sure that the needs of our home were met, even as she tackled the challenges of a full-time job as a school principal, Elder and volunteer in the ministry of our church. For more than twenty years she served in a too often neglected part of our community, Youth Ministry. She began first by working with the children in our Nursery Program, and in time, was promoted to the position of Executive Director of all the many components that make up our complex Youth/Young Adult Ministry.

As a committed leader, her responsibilities were not only to meet the needs of the preteens, teens and young adult in our youth programs, but also to address the requirements of the many adults who worked as volunteers. This meant that on any given night she was a counselor, a bank, a babysitter, a disciplinarian, a preacher, a cab driver and a miracle worker as she modeled for her staff what youth ministry was all about.

I watched my wife do all of this, knowing that much of what she was doing was not a natural part of who she was originally. Owing to some real challenges growing up, my wife was not inclined to be open to others. Quiet, a loner, forced to run away from home as a young teenager, she was the type of person who expected little from people in general. By the Grace of God she found Christ while still a teenager through the love of Bethel Gospel Assembly and a wonderful woman of God, Marie Donnadelle, who took her in and raised her as one of her own.

As a grown woman she may appreciate the occasional trip and meeting new, interesting people; but she is really like me, a home body. We both enjoy curling up with a book or catching an old movie on television. However, when called for the purposes of ministry, out comes this whole other person that goes the extra mile with people to help them navigate their way through the challenges of life. She does it all out of an authentic love placed there by God.

We have come to enjoy some of the fruit of our labor, as children we served over the years come back to Bethel with their own children, and tell us just how what we did for them at a critical point in their lives made the difference between life and death. As I witness the impact my wife has had on these lives, I realize again and again how blessed I am to have her by my side at this critical time of ministry. I can only stop to give God the praise for how He smiled upon me with this blessing.

Leaders must be prepared to go the extra mile! For many of those you seek to help, it will not be the initial contact you make with them, but how you persist and give of yourself through a Christian spirit of self denial that will cause them to finally let the light of Jesus Christ come through their door.

GALATIANS 6:8–10 says—

(8) *Those who live only to satisfy their own sinful desires will harvest the consequences of decay and death. But those who live to please the Spirit will harvest everlasting life from the Spirit.*

(9) *So don't get tired of doing what is good. Don't get discouraged and give up, for we will reap a harvest of blessing at the appropriate time.*

(10) *Whenever we have the opportunity, we should do good to everyone, especially to our Christian brothers and sisters.* (NLT)

EXPAND THE HORIZON!

When doing service in ministry, you are not done until you have prepared for the securing of the harvest and planned new strategies for increasing future yield.

Every endeavor should always ask the question, *What about tomorrow?* It may be in reference to a crusade with hundreds flooding the altar, or a powerful marriage conference with dozens of couples ready to confess their failures and make a fresh start. The question is, *What do we do next?* In fact, what do you do if you fall short of the goals you set for your service? After the investment of time and treasure, if you do not fulfill all your mission goals, your team will look to you for explanation and direction. What do you do then? When we do service for the Lord we come to see that God's plans always extends themselves into the next phase, tomorrow! We can never be finished; we can only carry on into the next phase of His design. A great portion of scripture is found in John 21. In making the point as to how we are to approach either of the above scenarios I would like to draw attention to that impetuous disciple of Christ, Peter.

JOHN 21:3–14 says—

(3) Simon Peter said, "I'm going fishing." "We'll come, too," they all said. So they went out in the boat, but they caught nothing all night.

(4) At dawn the disciples saw Jesus standing on the beach, but they couldn't see who he was.

(5) He called out, "Friends, have you caught any fish?" "No," they replied.

(6) Then he said, "Throw out your net on the right hand side of the boat, and you'll get plenty of fish!" So they did, and they couldn't draw in the net because there were so many fish in it.

(7) Then the disciple whom Jesus loved said to Peter, "It is the LORD!" When Simon Peter heard that it was the LORD, he put on his tunic (for he had stripped for work), jumped into the water, and swam ashore.

(8) The others stayed with the boat and pulled the loaded net to the shore, for they were only out about three hundred feet.

(9) When they got there, they saw that a charcoal fire was burning and fish were frying over it, and there was bread.

(10) "Bring some of the fish you've just caught," Jesus said.

(11) So Simon Peter went aboard and dragged the net to the shore. There were 153 large fish, and yet the net hadn't torn.

(12) "Now come and have some breakfast!" Jesus said. And no one dared ask him if he really was the Lord because they were sure of it.

(13) Then Jesus served them the bread and the fish.

(14) This was the third time Jesus had appeared to his disciples since he had been raised from the dead. (NLT)

The portion of the text in question brings readily to mind the occasion i

Luke 5:4-11 when, after toiling all night the disciples had nothing to show for it, but were then humbled by Jesus when He told them to "go fish." Humoring their great teacher, they were amazed when they caught so many fish their boat began to sink. Then and there Christ caught their attention and they eventually became His followers.

Now, once again, Peter takes the lead as they were waiting for the next shoe to drop after the death and resurrection of their Master. The waiting was too much for Peter, so he declared, "I'm going fishing!" Following his lead, they all went, and after toiling all night were ready to toss it in and quit. Just then a stranger appears on the far shore with a question.

"Friends, did you catch anything?" After they admitted to catching nothing, He instructed them to make an adjustment. Years earlier, they may have ignored such backseat driving, but having been humbled by recent events and years of following their Master, they readily agreed. While the professional in them may have suggested another kind of response, their experience in Christ had taught them to "never say never," and they went back to work, following His suggestion.

Their expanded horizon had taught them not to quit, but to stay open to seeing the value in a fresh approach when confronted with challenging conditions. This would be especially important later when, after the Pentecost, the church of God began to grow and a fierce wave of persecution hit the church. They remained flexible and secure as they found their spiritual nets being filled with Gentiles, newly baptized in the Holy Ghost. Seeing the supernatural abundance of fresh souls, they recognized that God had simply given them a new sea to catch some more fish.

In our own endeavors we must be open to the teaching experience that may begin when we are humbled by circumstances before God and man. When an endeavor has been launched based on our own flawed understanding, it is easy for us to want to just bury it, to abandon it as just one of those things. But if you truly believe the flawed plan is God at work, then stick around with Him and discover the lessons you are meant to draw from the

117

experience. Remain firm and through your faith in Christ, believe in the miraculous working hand of God reaching forward to retrieve His glory from difficult circumstances.

Now take note of JOHN 21:7 where it states—
Then the disciple whom Jesus loved said to Peter, "It is the LORD!"
When Simon Peter heard that it was the LORD, he put on his tunic
(for he had stripped for work), jumped into the water, and swam
ashore. (NLT)

The Verse states how Peter "had stripped to work," but once he heard from John that Jesus had come, his feeling was "Aha? Now the work is done and it is time to rest in Jesus." But as soon as he reaches his master he receives the next command from the Lord, "Bring some of the fish you just caught." Peter went back to do as he was commanded and found the net filled with fish to the brim, so full it could not be pulled into the boat. Yet it had not broken. What Peter brought to the Lord was that which the Lord had ordained to be added to what had already been prepared.

Jesus had shown up, and they had taken in quite a haul, but the work was not yet done. Something had to be done with that haul, and there was still a role for Peter to play. Many times, after a great expenditure of time, effort and resources, we say to ourselves, "Job well done. Let's celebrate and move on to conquer fresh territories." But the job is not over until you understand and execute God's plan for the fish. In this portion of the text, Peter was called to bring some of the "153 large fishes" to what the Lord had already processed on the shore. By this act, Peter was not merely adding to the number, but expanding the function of the disciples' catch, thus fulfilling the purpose of the exercise.

I am afraid that many of our church outreach efforts have majored in numbers, but fallen short in terms of the discipling of these individuals into their place in Christ Jesus. We fail to prepare New Believer classes to in tiate them into the significance of our worship experience. We also fail to adjust the attitudes of the saints to recognize the importance of making these new believers an active part of our church community. As we mentioned several chapters earlier, it is important to answer the question, "Who will clean the fish?' It is important that we don't quit our task before it is complete. If it did not go as planned, what adjustments does Christ need us to make to bring in a strong harvest?

If there has been a wonderful response, then praise God, but what comes next? How are we to advance the experience to the next level in Christ's purposes? If it was a success, then we must believe that every single part of that harvest belongs to God, and that He is able to preserve it and keep it in our care. In spite of the weight of the catch, the Bible says, "the nets did not break"! Whatever happens in the course of time to the souls we are blessed to receive by God, it is critical that we know and perform our part in bringing them to the spiritual shores of salvation and discipleship.

In the next section, God's plans for Peter could be more clearly understood in terms of a personal calling and purpose:

JOHN 21:15–17 says—

(15) *After breakfast Jesus said to Simon Peter, "Simon son of John, do you love me more than these?" "Yes, LORD," Peter replied, "you know I love you." "Then feed my lambs," Jesus told him.*

(16) *Jesus repeated the question: "Simon son of John, do you love me?" "Yes, LORD," Peter said, "you know I love you." "Then take care of my sheep," Jesus said.*

(17) *Once more he asked him, "Simon son of John, do you love me?" Peter was grieved that Jesus asked the question a third time. He said, "LORD, you know everything. You know I love you." Jesus said, "Then feed my sheep." (NLT)*

have both heard and taught from this portion of scripture several times. It really is a great lesson, bringing out many different concepts of ministry.

One aspect connects to the earlier section outlining to Peter that the mission was not over.

Beyond challenging Peter about the quality of his love for the Lord (in the Greek you see the word play between Christ's *agape* love and Peter's *phileo* love response in a discourse that, unlike some scholars, I do see as significant), He was also challenging Peter to undertake his mission as He says to Peter, "If you truly love me more than these, then go to work to feed the lambs and the sheep," telling him to take care of the harvest and bring them to a new level of relationship in Him (Jesus Christ).

Here I believe Christ is speaking of the new converts, the faithful disciples and the other disciples that will become part of the sheepfold in Christ; the new ("the lambs"), the familiar ("my sheep"), and the other ("the Sheep"). These are the ones we will continue to meet in the marketplace, in our neighborhood, and in our travels overseas. They are the ones who will look different, talk different, and even think different about some things, but they will come to accept the same faith in the Lord Jesus Christ as we believe: that He is the Lord over all our traditions, our denominations, our color. Paul draws this point out in the Book of Ephesians, Chapter 4:9-13:

> (9) ...*Christ first came down to the lowly world in which we live.*
> (10) *The same One who came down is the One who ascended higher than all the heavens, so that His rule might fill the entire universe.*
> (11) *He is the One who gave these gifts to the church: the apostles, the prophets, the evangelists and the pastors and teachers.*
> (12) *Their responsibility is to equip God's people to do his work and build up the church, the body of Christ,*
> (13) *until we come to such unity in our faith and knowledge of God's Son that we will be mature and full grown in the LORD, measuring up to the full stature of Christ.* (NLT)

The King James Version uses the phrase, "Edifying of the body of Christ, which in the Greek means to build or expand the body. This expansion comes through a trained army of believers who faithfully set out to win new converts into Christ's fold. These new converts in time will be equipped to become the next set of disciples actively engaged in the work; setting out to win new converts into the fold.

There are some of us that take the theme, "Resting in Jesus" to the extreme. We have come to Jesus with joy, and declare, "Cares all past, home at last." This is true to a great extent, but we will not find that ultimate peace until this life is over. In the meantime, God has called us to be His "traveling sales force," extolling the virtue of what we have found to be true in Christ Jesus. As much as we want to be close to Jesus and sit at his feet like Peter, Jesus commands us to sail back into the water to help bring in the next catch! The final portion in John 21:18–22 seems to beg the question, *How long do you expect me to stay here in this kind of labor?*

JOHN 21:18-22 says—

(18) *"The truth is, when you were young, you were able to do as you liked and go wherever you wanted to. But when you are old, you will stretch out your hands, and others will direct you and take you where you don't want to go."*

(19) *Jesus said this to let him know what kind of death he would die to glorify God. Then Jesus told him, "Follow me."*

(20) *Peter turned around and saw the disciple Jesus loved following them—the one who had leaned over to Jesus during supper and asked, "LORD, who among us will betray you?"*

(21) *Peter asked Jesus, "What about him, LORD?"*

(22) *Jesus replied, "If I want him to remain alive until I return, what is that to you? You follow me."*

(23) *So the rumor spread among the community of believers that that disciple wouldn't die. But that isn't what Jesus said at all. He only said, "If I want him to remain alive until I return, what is that to*

you?" (NLT)

The Lord, anticipating Peter's question, speaks a prophetic word over his life and gives him a final command, "Follow me." He seems to be saying, "Don't worry about it. You don't understand all the details, and there will be some real challenges, but you have the right heart and you are shooting at the right target. So just do it!" Likewise, we are to be ever vigilant as we plan for the growth of our Master's church by making provision for follow-up ministries, and those ministries' participations in rising up, training and releasing new disciples, new disciples that will faithfully understand the command, 'Til Death Do You S.H.O.P.

This book is a testimonial to the real life expression of God manifested through a committed congregation active in one of the most exciting battlegrounds in the world. I pray that these words will excite your imagination and stimulate your spiritual appetite for the wonderful opportunity awaiting all the spiritual shoppers out there.

Oh, one last thing. "This Store called Earth closes in..." sooner than you think!

PASSING THE MANTLE: THE RACE CONTINUES
BIOGRAPHICAL SKETCHES OF THE THREE PASTORS
OF BETHEL GOSPEL ASSEMBLY

Rev.. James Barzey

Bishop Dr. Ezra N. Williams

Photo Credit: Shahar Azran

Bishop Carlton T. Brown

JAMES BARZEY
SENIOR PASTOR 1924–1965

During the developmental phase of the ministry, Lillian Kraeger would often appeal for help to her friend, Bishop George Phillips, President of the United Pentecostal Council of the Assemblies of God, headquartered in Cambridge, Massachusetts. This notable leader would make monthly trips to New York to assist her in giving leadership to the Bethel church; however Mother Kraeger (as she was affectionately called) understood that God's hand was definitely on this group of young people in Harlem. She also realized that the time had come for the church to continue in its development under leadership raised from the rank and file. It was towards this end she began to direct her prayers.

Born in the 1890's on the Island of St. Kitts, James Barzey eventually migrated to the United States, settling into fellowship with the fledgling Bethel Gospel Assembly by 1922. He proved himself to be a strong and dependable asset to the church. By 1924, Lillian Kraeger determined that it was time for the church to formally fill the office of Senior Pastor, and elections were held with Elder Barzey emerging as the first Pastor of Bethel Gospel Assembly.

Standing at six feet, three inches tall, Pastor Barzey was a muscular young man with piercing eyes and a booming voice. A man used to commanding the attention and respect of those around him, Barzey was well-suited for the challenge of securing the support and maintaining the spiritual discipline within a congregation faced with radical changes in the social and economic landscape over the next three decades.

While being an adherent to the Pentecostal faith, there was no mistaking the old-time religious virtues that were entrenched in this man of God. While the Harlem of that day was immersed in the often risqué verses and sounds of the blues and jazz of that era, along with the liberating political tomes of the various black writers and community activists based in the

"Black Capital" of America, this devout, old-fashioned minister from the Caribbean charted a course for the youth of the church that was conservative in both its religious and social expressions.

The type of church music sung during worship remained true to the Hymns and acceptable brand of Caribbean flavored choruses popular in his youth, while his politics honored the Pauline teaching that it is God who places "the sword in the hands of government." In spite of the earlier rejection that resulted in the birth of Bethel and the racial discrimination present even in Harlem, there was a natural resistance within Bethel against resentment towards the whites. This platform was informed through Biblical teaching and the Caribbean mind-set that diminished the overall impact of racism.

His simple, yet inspirational preaching and leadership proved to be critical to the survival of the church through the depression and war years that followed his ascendancy to the pastorate. For the Bethel church community, the next two decades came furnished with its own testimonies of the miraculous power of God upon its anointed body of believers. Under the leadership of Pastor Barzey, Bethel moved into what was known as Father Divine Kingdom, 36-38 West 123rd Street. A stately landmark building on the corner of Lenox Avenue in Harlem, it was four stories tall and had a full basement.

Used as a meeting hall by the celebrated and controversial Black leader of the Twenties and Thirties, the Reverend Major Jealous Divine, a.k.a, "Father Divine," just prior to its purchase by Bethel, the building had six apartments on the upper floors that were used to house some of the families of the church including Pastor Barzey himself, while the meeting hall/sanctuary could seat 100–125 people.

Without question, Lillian Kraeger's influence in the matter of race cannot be overlooked. The long memories of some of the children who were seen but not heard (now in their late seventies and eighties) recall comments attributed to the matriarch that she preferred lighter-skinned negroes over their darker skinned counterparts. While notions persist that there may have been some negative levels of Mother Kraeger's loving contribution towards the establishment and nurturing of the Assembly during its early development, her overall contribution and devotion to the church is beyond question.

The Bethel of the Barzey years can best be described as a predominantly Caribbean immigrant, first generation church consisting of large families raised in two parent homes. Being a proud lot, most would never characterized themselves as poor, as the fathers would hold two or three low-paying jobs, and the mothers (who may have earned a dollar or two doing odd sewing or cleaning jobs) stayed at home to raise the kids and perform miracles with the fathers' meager paychecks and whatever was cooking in the pots.

Yet when you talk to any of these children from the Barzey era, they always recount these years with great fondness and appreciation, even if not for the man himself, who was more feared than revered. His authoritarian manner was greatly appreciated by their parents who regarded his word as law. The collective stand Pastor Barzey and the parents took against the pleasures and perils of the Harlem streets of the Thirties through the early Sixties saved many young lives in the congregation.

Having finally paid off its mortgage in 1965, the membership of approximately one hundred, debt-free, church property owners, who existed under solid and well-seasoned leadership, seemed poised to make an even greater contribution to the work of God.

EZRA N. WILLIAMS
SENIOR PASTOR 1966–2000

With the sudden passing of Pastor Barzey, a thirty-six-year old trumpet playing, youth loving, commode cleaning bus driver was called to leave a secure position with the MTA to lead a reduced number of a somewhat demoralized Bethelites into a measure of ministry that appeared to be far beyond his ability. But still, the man that God called was one whose history was steeped in Bethel lore.

Back in 1923, Lillian Kraeger and some of the saints had been invited to the apartment of Gertrude and Venus Williams, two young siblings interested in hearing more about the Lord Jesus Christ. But the other occupants, Livingston, Gertrude's husband, and his older brother Wesley, Venus' husband, had other plans for that evening that certainly did not included the Gospel. As Bishop Williams related it:

"The tension had grown to the point where Wesley, the older and more outspoken of the two husbands, demanded that the two sisters remove themselves from the premises or face the consequences. Then there was a knock on the door—Lillian Kraeger had arrived with her gospel posse, and in the true British posture of the time, both Wesley and Livingston stood on their best behavior and graciously received their new guests."

Before she left that evening Lillian claimed four new converts to the Lord and Bethel Gospel Assembly. In time, Venus and Wesley would be responsible for the planting of the Georgetown church on the island of St. Vincent where four branches of Bethel Gospel Assembly exist today. An even greater contribution was made by the future Deacon Livingston and his wife Gertrude, as their eldest son would in time become the second Pastor of Bethel Gospel Assembly.

Raised in Bethel Gospel Assembly from birth, Ezra's sermons were often colored with wonderful illustrations from his experiences running through the streets of Harlem as a boy, training as a leader in the military during the Korean War, and his study of people during his twelve years driving a New York City bus. As a young man he became the youngest member of the church board, this status giving him the ignoble task of vacuuming the floors and cleaning the toilets. Those experiences, along with his grooming as head of the youth group, both in Bethel and the United Pentecostal Counsel of Assemblies of God, Eastern District, helped make him a wise shepherd. Filled with a loving spirit and drive for excellence for his Lord and Savior Jesus Christ, he emerged as a great leader who carried the message of the gospel far and wide.

While the economics and social conditions of his time did not make the climb to college possible, young Ezra excelled as an apt Bible student brimming with promise. During those days when Seminary was not as readily accessible for economic reasons, Ezra was able to achieve Biblical scholarship at the renowned Manhattan Bible Institute under the presidency of Dr. James Boyce, both prior to and directly after his ascendancy to the pastorate of Bethel Gospel Assembly after the death of Pastor Barzey in 1965.

His distinctive blend of experience presented Bethel with a thirty-seven-year-old visionary having a heart for the people of God throughout the world. His entire being burned bright with a sense of purpose—his belief that God had given him and the people he led a mandate to share that love wherever the Lord may take them.

By the late Sixties, Bethel had stepped up the pace in sharing the Word of God in the streets of Harlem and had become actively involved in Crusades in the Caribbean. Bishop Williams, now seventy-nine, often speaks of the many promises the Lord used to encourage him during many a difficult and trying season. One such promise that came to pass early in his ministry took place soon after he had began his leadership over the church.

Recognized as a prankster during his years in school and in the church, many of the senior saints doubted this young man had either the ability or the discipline to lead the hurting congregation into better times. They held great reverence for the late Pastor Barzey, and when they looked at this comparatively small, five-foot-nine-inch, trumpet-playing youth leader, there was nothing in his demeanor or loving nature that inspired positive comparisons with their fallen hero.

Immediately after Ezra Williams became Pastor, many saints left what they deemed to be a sinking ship. Undaunted, sure in the knowledge that God had called him, his wife Dorthea, and his three children Mark, Debbie and Allison into the Kingdom for just such a time as this, Ezra sought God for direction. He immediately received a command and a promise, "Sow abroad and reap at home." Others counseled against this strategy, saying that he had heard wrong. "Better to secure your home front first before launching out to unknown waters," they told him, but on the first of many such occasions, Ezra stood firm in his faith and conviction, trusted God, and reaped the reward in the end. A Rational Radical indeed.

The late Sixties and early Seventies witnessed a new era within Bethel Gospel Assembly as its pulpit was carried abroad and into the streets of Harlem. Inspired by the faith and energy of this young, charismatic leader, a new wave of support promoted the work of the ministry. Seasoned by many years of hard work, these years ushered in the era of the second and third generations of the founding families of the church. This new group of supporters numbered many who would go on to college and return to the church with a renewed hunger to serve God in ways unrealized by the previous generation. With their ranks bolstered by a new fresh wave of new converts, Bethel rallied under the leadership of Pastor Williams and rose to meet the challenges facing the ministry.

By this time the Crusade Teams consisted mostly of people from the ages of seventeen to twenty-eight, and they traveled with Pastor Ezra to places such as Montserrat and Aruba, while those that could not travel abroad, stood shoulder to shoulder with him in the streets of Harlem and the South Bronx, ministering to gang leaders, prostitutes, alcoholics and drug addicts. These parishioners witnessed hundreds of lives being transformed and new churches established abroad. Being true to His Word, the church at home began to experience a radical growth that could only be attributed to God.

Bethel's whole emphasis was now on World Evangelism. It was clear this emerging view could be directly attributed to Pastor Williams' concern for mission when as a child of ten he watched his Uncle Wesley form a one man Mission Committee to support his wife and cousins in their work in St. Vincent in 1937.

He always felt that God had a better plan than separating a husband and a wife due to lack of financial support. These thoughts never left him, and so in a few short years, along with the supporting leadership of Mission Director Ruth Onukwue, MD, they raised the Missions budget from $12,000 in the late Sixties (with membership of 90–125) to $150,000 per year by 1979 (with membership of about 200).

Pastor Williams' gifts as a leader are widely recognized and highly regarded to this day. It is a documented fact that after being drafted during the Korean War, his swift actions during an ugly racial incident in the barracks averted a race riot at a training camp in Texas. He was immediately rewarded with new orders to report to Officer Candidate School. After being met there with great racial prejudice, Sergeant Williams' demonstrated poise under pressure led directly to his assignment to train new recruits for the duration of the war!

Shortly after becoming Pastor at Bethel he was chosen to serve as the National President of the United Pentecostal Council of the Assemblies of God, and did so with distinction from 1969–1981. He was so loved and honored by that organization that he was installed as Eastern District Bishop in 1986, and then National Bishop a short time later, succeeding the late Bishop Roderick R. Caesar, Sr. He faithfully served in that capacity until 1995 when Bethel left the UPCAG to pursue other ministry opportunities through Urban Global Missions Alliance (founded for the promotion of Missions by Bishop Williams in 1997).

Never forgetting his own experiences in the gang-ridden streets of

Harlem in the Thirties and Forties, Bishop Williams accepted a post on the Board of Directors of Teen Challenge. He served faithfully throughout the Seventies, Eighties and into the early Nineties, at that time the only non-Assemblies of God leader asked to serve on that Board.

In the spring of 2002, in recognition of his outstanding service to the Harlem community and his contribution to the efforts of World Evangelism, Bishop Williams received an honorary Doctorate from the Alliance Theological Seminary, Nyack, New York. It was a proud moment in the life of a man who was once told by his High School principal, "You will never amount to anything!"

Acknowledging the special move of God in the Bethel Ministry during the late Seventies, as evidenced through the radical growth in membership along with his personal ministry; Bishop Williams led Bethel in the acquisition and mammoth renovation of its current facility on 120th Street between Fifth and Madison. During 1982 through 1984, James Fenimore Cooper Junior High School was an abandoned and vandalized building. Built in 1942, it was closed in 1975 and put up for auction by the City in 1982. By coincidence, its very first year was marked by many a prank perpetrated upon an unsuspecting student body by one of its seniors, Ezra N. Williams. These pranks often led to him becoming an unwilling guest in the Principal's office. In 1982 at the age of 55, he became the occupant of the very office that witnessed the pronouncement that he "would never succeed in life!"

For the next sixteen years Bethel continued to expand its borders, establishing ministries both at home and abroad, including such ministries as the Beth Hark Counseling Center and the Bethel Discipleship Program, a twenty-four/seven, eighteen month residential spiritual development program for men. As the Church continued to grow there could be no mistake that its understanding of purpose revolved around the Mission's mandate, taught so often by this man of God. This eternal message, found in all the four Gospels, is best summed up by the words, "Go and tell!"

CARLTON T. BROWN
SENIOR PASTOR 2000–PRESENT

In 1980 as a young deacon in the church, Bishop Williams informed me that the Lord had instructed him to elevate me to Associate Pastor alongside two others. When my initial reaction was to refuse him, I was quickly reminded by God that one year earlier, during a crisis in my life, God Himself had informed me of this call to ministry. By making me aware of this call, God made me understand that I must submit, and trust Him to perfect in me those ministry gifts I could not accept to be part of my life.

Acknowledging this to be a true encounter with God, and with the loving support of my wife, I acquiesced, and in July, 1981 both Pastor Gordon Williams (my current Associate Pastor) and I were ordained into the ministry. Incorporating my training as an educator and supervisor, I soon tackled various responsibilities in the Missions (where it has been my distinct pleasure to be mentored by Dr. Ruth Onukwue, MD, a true gift of God to Bethel for over 30 years), Youth, and Christian Education departments. It has been my privilege to initiate various programs and organizational innovations within the ministry throughout the Eighties and Nineties.

That simple affirmative answer to the call of God resulted in twenty years of service as a Sunday School teacher, followed by thirteen years of Service as the Director and Minister of Christian Education. Ten years of leadership over the Youth Ministry of the church resulted in the dramatic transformation of the department. We are excited to see many of the initiatives birthed during that time still flourishing to this day.

As National Missions Director for the UPCAG from 1990–1995 I was given the wonderful opportunity to develop and lead several Missions' Conferences and Crusade initiatives for that organization. It was during this time that I was blessed to work closely with Dr. Edgar Lashley, former Pastor of Ebenezer Gospel Church and the National President of UPCAG from 1989 through 1995. Dr. Lashley's vast experience as a leader and businessman was to have a great impact on me, giving me a greater dimension of invaluable insight. It was to my great advantage to serve in this capacity until Bethel's departure from that organization in 1995.

In those years as Bethel's Associate Pastor and the Director of Missions of the United Pentecostal Council of the Assemblies of God, I traveled extensively around the world serving as a conference speaker and Crusade leader and organizer. We were blessed to make trips to many nations, including Nigeria, Kenya, South Africa, Panama, Jamaica, Trinidad, Barbados and Aruba, as well as a number of different sites around the United States. I am very grateful to have had the opportunity to serve the Lord so widely.

On December 7, 1999, Bishop Ezra Williams presented me to the assembled membership of Bethel Gospel Assembly to succeed him as the Senior Pastor and Chairman of the Board of Bethel Gospel Assembly, Inc. By pledged agreement of the Assembly and with my wife Lorna at my side, I was installed as Senior Pastor on the fourth Sunday of February, 2000.

Throughout the ensuing years, God has proven himself faithful to Lorna and I and our two children Justin and Carla, while Bethel Gospel Assembly continues to grow and remains faithful to its roots; an overarching sense of duty to God to spread the gospel near and far.

Recognizing the importance of spreading the Good News by sowing abroad, we have faithfully followed the lead of the Holy Spirit by planting missionaries and churches overseas. At the same time, we have also launched ministries on the local front, having established a total of eight churches in the states of New York, New Jersey, Georgia and Virginia. In response to the request for oversight and accountability to several ministries around the world and those which we've had the privilege to plant in 2002, we founded the Bethel Gospel Global Assemblies, which I serve as Bishop and General Overseer.

With the help of the Lord we have also prepared new Men's and Women's programs, and Bethel's Christian Education ministry has support ed church communities around the city. Our Youth Ministry has been expanded to offer a safe haven for youth from the community as well as the Bethel family. Our goal is to transform an entire community. We do so by charging our membership with the responsibility to reach out, one to one, to individuals and present to them the ultimate experience one can have, a personal relationship with Jesus Christ.

In 2004, Bethel launched its first Northeast Regional Great Commission Conference. Since early 1971, Bethel has held a yearly local Missions' Conference that involves the entire Bethel community in learning about the call of God to forward World Evangelism. Since this expansion The Great Commission Conference in 2005 included the Caribbean as well as the Northeast region, representing an investment by this ministry to promote the cause of Missions among ministries open to receive that message. Missions cannot be an optional item on any church's agenda; *it is the agenda of the church*. Yet it has been shown that fewer than ninety percent of the churches in North America have a viable mission's board and program.

With many initiatives both local and global, Bethel Gospel Assembly stands committed to fulfilling its assignments in the cause of Jesus Christ. These initiatives include:

♦ Broadening our presence on the mission field by establishing at least 20 missionary families in Africa, Asia, the Caribbean/South America and Europe by the year 2020.

♦ The expansion of our Harmony Christian Academy located on the South African Harmony Estates complex to go from 130 students to over 350 students, along with the addition of an orphanage and training center within the next two years.

♦ The completion of our housing complex that sits atop our new sanctuary, with both slated for dedication in 2009. Our plans are to use these rental units to not only provide affordable housing in the high price New York City market, but to also establish a funding stream for future missions projects both home and abroad.

• Shortly after the dedication of our new facilities we will proceed with the conversion of our old Sanctuary into a theatre complex for the purposes of housing long running Christian oriented productions just 5 blocks west and 2 blocks over from the world famous Apollo Theatre.

• And, we are currently at work extending the reach of our recently established, state-of-the-art Becoming God's Answer Bookstore (named after our radio program in NYC) to include Internet sales, and other creative projects.

Through these endeavors and so much more, it is our determination to faithfully remain "A Loving, Learning and Launching church," meeting the needs of people around the world with both the message and demonstration of the Lordship of Jesus Christ. May the Lord bless you all!

APPENDIX II
THE PACE CURRICULUM

Faithful to the promise that God had given Bishop Williams—"Sow abroad and you will reap at home," Bethel experienced rapid growth in the late Seventies and the Eighties, necessitating the move to its present quarters on the square block of property on 120th Street between Madison and Fifth.

As a result of this surge in membership, we have also experienced one of the major drawbacks to being a church of a thousand-plus members—the tendency for some of us to get lost in the crowd. Despite having twenty or more deacons, the reality is that the deacons cannot keep track of and be accountable for their overwhelming membership lists of as many as forty to sixty people each.

One solution to this common problem is small, home group studies. Acts, Chapter 2 speaks of the radical growth of the church, and prior to the incorporation of Deacons, it was in home meetings that the growth was cultivated and secured, as ministry took place on a regular basis in both the Temple and "from house to house."(Acts 2:46)

In the spring of 2000, the Lord directed me, as the newly installed Senior Pastor of Bethel Gospel Assembly, to incorporate a series of church-wide home cell meetings—called Clusters—as a part of our fifty days of prayer and fasting. By rough estimates, over 60% of our members (which is the acceptable support rate for home cell meetings) joined in the exercise with positive results. Since that time, we have been awaiting clearance from the Lord to add a permanent Home Bible study structure to the ministry of the church. That time has come!

The call for Home Cell ministry at Bethel was first suggested by Pastor Ezra N. Williams in the late Seventies and early Eighties. It was during the time when Christendom was awash with discussion of the Pastor Yongi Choi church growth phenomenon in South Korea and the Larry Lea ministry in Texas. Cell groups have become firmly established as the most effective means for managing what would come to be known as "mega-churches." This term has come to describe churches that total more than two thousand members; but it should be noted that any church totaling two hundred or more is considered a large church.

With the assistance of the late Reverend Faith Brown, I reviewed material in preparation for the adaptation of a Home Cell program designed for the unique conditions of New York City. While Home Cell programs have met with great success in various places around the country, New York had not boasted such results. As time went on, Bethel experienced several significant changes and appreciable growth in numbers. Plans for the implementation of the Home Cell program were set aside, yet not completely abandoned.

In the early Nineties, the leadership of Bethel were invited to share fellowship with Pastor Tim Keller and some of his leadership at Redeemer Presbyterian church, known as the "Church without Walls." The scholarship and leadership skills of this tremendous man of God have not only resulted in the establishing of a mega-church, but have maintained the spiritual integrity of the ministry by establishing one of the largest Home Cell programs in the Northeast.

A wise professor from the Educational Psychology graduate program at NYU once said to our class, "Don't spend time trying to reinvent the wheel; there are good programs at work out there. Research, review and use them." Much of what God has given us in the PACE program at Bethel comes from my early studies from twenty years ago and a careful review of the administrative and training structure found in the powerful program launched by Redeemer. While we have adapted a measure of the structure used in the Redeemer model, the greater part comes from the heart of what is the philosophy of ministry of Bethel Gospel Assembly and the vision that God has given me for 21st Century ministry.

Much has happened as a result of the 9/11 tragedy, including the great need for ministry built on a more intense level of spiritually-based relationship. In the midst of a strange brew of spiritual openness and depravity, the church has to produce empowered believers who are equipped to share the Gospel both in word and in practice. This can only be realized through lives that are immersed in the essentials of our faith.

WHY PACE?

Pace addresses the need to promote the Good News among the community of believers and into the world that God has assigned us to reach. PACE stands for:

PRAYER
ACCOUNTABILITY
CURRICULUM
EVANGELISM

PRAYER

The reality is the vital importance of prayer is often overlooked in the success of the church. While much time is spent in meetings, fundraising, rehearsals, and in the development and execution of programs, it is the spiritual army which spends more valuable time on its knees that wins the day.

The Bible states that we ought to pray and not faint. This is a critical component to any successful ministry and each believer must be both exposed to and practiced in the use of this valuable spiritual resource. Heartfelt and focused prayer will reduce the time spent counseling, fundraising and running down our prodigal sons and daughters.

ACCOUNTABILITY

Deuteronomy 6:4-9 speaks to the surrendering of our hearts to the single true God, and by virtue of that immersion we are taught to teach our Christian values to our children:

> 1) In your home: Follow up on your family altar, family meetings and other Christian family interaction opportunities.
>
> 2) When you walk by the way of Christ you show who you are in your community and your social dealings.
>
> 3) When you lie down and rise up: model your study and communication with God.
>
> 4) Bind your devotions to your eyes: Write them, exhibit them, memorize them and let them be exhibited as the direct evidence of your devotion in the Lord in your home by modeling them.

This process brings about the promotion, cultivation and perpetuation of divine truth and revelation within a spiritual community. The immersion of the community in the knowledge, understanding and execution (practice) of the will of God fortifies the efforts of the church to transform the community at large, preventing recidivism and facilitating spiritual awakening.

Bible dictionaries such as Easton's and Holman tell us that the Custom of Orthodox Jewish men has been to copy four sections from the law (Exodus 13:1–10 and 13:11–16; Deuteronomy 6:4–9 and 11:13–21) and put these passages in leather cases on straps and bind them to their left arms and onto their foreheads during morning prayer. They also put Deuteronomy 6:4–5 and 11:13–20 in a metal or glass case and affix it to the right-hand door post of every entrance to their homes.

Jesus rebuked the Pharisees not because they wore the phylacteries, but because they displayed them ostentatiously while denying the message. They exalted the trappings of religion over the condition of the heart even though God is more concerned about how we improve the condition of the heart than any outer sign of apparent devotion.

Our effectiveness as believers is enhanced when we seek the assistance of the Holy Spirit and the mentoring of experienced counselors who can assist us to internalize the Word. It is not our intention to adopt an external list of rules and procedures. In truth, none of us are really good at that, we automatically look for short cuts. But to realize divine truth in our hearts in a manner that results in real, lasting change, we require the assistance of our Bethel brothers and sisters who are steeped in the Word. It has been said, "The heart never forgets!"

MATTHEW 22:37–40 says—

(37) *Love the Lord your God with all your heart and with all your soul and all your mind.*

(38) *This is the first and greatest commandment.*

(39) *And the second is like it: "Love your neighbor as yourself."*

(40) *All the Law and the Prophets hang on these two commandments.*

(NIV)

It is God's choice that this heart process be established in partnership within the Church community, not in isolation! The goal of the church is to ensure that each member takes advantage of the mentoring processes the church makes available to aid their spiritual pursuits. Only in community can the individual member's spiritual growth be assured, as the spiritual path of the isolated Christian is beset by many perils that can only be avoided with the help of the church's spiritual assets.

The basic system of accountability used in Bethel has been achieved through the empowerment of the Deacon Board. These men and woman have been a great blessing in Bethel, helping the Pastor and ministers to stay abreast of the needs of the Church body. Each member is assigned to a deacon, and each member is expected to call them in time of crisis. Due to the tremendous demands of a growing church that deploys twenty or more deacons, the reality is accountability has been overextended, as each deacon's membership list surpasses forty members and may total as many as sixty.

PACE offers opportunities for the appropriation of positive and practiced Christian values as a lifestyle, through the regular and intimate support of the family of God.

CURRICULUM

This element speaks to the need to study to show oneself approved unto God. There is a need within the church community to build itself corporately in the Word of God.

Deuteronomy 6:4 represents the beginning of the most important phrase in the Jewish Book of the Law. It is the Shema, meaning, "To Hear intelligently with the purpose of obedience," the essential creed of Judaism, used to open every Jewish service and the first Scripture that every Jewish child commits to memory. "Hear, O Israel: The Lord our God, the Lord is one!" God = Elohim, a plural noun of unstated number that to my mind automatically defaults to the number 3, which equals the Trinity!

Jesus identifies it as the first and greatest Commandment; the bottom line to the Ten Commandments and everything else as in Matthew 22:37–40. This Scripture speaks to the whole of man—

Heart = Seat of mind and will.
Soul = Life and vitality.
Might = Strength.

142

So we make a total presentation to the community of our emotions, thoughts and actions and learn how to love God through obedience and a committed lifestyle wholly pleasing to the Lord.

We are commanded to teach it: (discipline or disciple it = systematic training or subjection to authority; especially the training of the mental, moral and physical powers of the individual by instruction and exercise. The result of this: creating the habit of obedience. As per Shannan: to point or pierce—to inculcate). To teach it, we must submit ourselves to learn it! You can only learn it by experience! "It shall be in your heart!"

At Bethel Gospel Assembly, our Master Life, MP3 Men's Purity and Commitment classes, Discipleship classes and Bible College are just a part of the efforts that have been successful in bringing us into loving compliance to what Jesus underscores as the bottom line of faith! It is our desire that PACE will join this honor roll of small group opportunities that builds strong Christian character and successful Christian living before our Lord.

EVANGELISM

This speaks to the sharing of the Word of God to every people and group in accordance to the Great Commission. As I recently preached in a message referring to an incident with a small boy in a predominately Moslem nation, the sharing of the gospel is, "One beggar telling another beggar where he got the bread he now is willing to share with Him!"

The excellent material on small groups from the Redeemer Presbyterian Church Manual on Home Meetings, gives a wonderful commentary on the value of these types of meetings. It states:

"The context for a gospel-centered life is never merely individual. The gospel creates a new community, a unique community. 'One of the immediate changes that the gospel makes is grammatical: we instead of I; our instead of my; us instead of me.' (Eugene Peterson, *Reversed Thunder*). This kind of new community is not an optional thing, an 'extra' for the

Christian; instead it's part of the overall purposes of God's Kingdom."

A new community is both the goal of the gospel and also the means of spreading the gospel. God's promise in salvation is to create His "holy nation", a people that dwell with Him forever. "I will be your God and you will be my people." (Leviticus 26:12, Jeremiah 30:22) Christians, who are eternally united to Christ, are therefore eternally united to one another. We all are ministers of the gospel for the sake of one another. Since our culture knows very little about true community, we will have to work hard at following a Biblical vision.

What is the Biblical vision, what does true community look like? We are to be:

1) An accepting community that reflects the grace we've been given from Christ.

2) A holy community that urges one another to live God-pleasing lives.

3) A truth-telling community that is free to repent and free to allow others to repent because of the gospel.

4) An encouraging community that builds one another up on a day-to-day basis.

5) A generous community willing to sacrifice, that gladly spends its life and wealth on the needs of others.

6) A suffering community that loves and forgives others even when they harm us.

Our goal is to experience conversion growth in the church, some of which will come by way of invitation to family, friends and acquaintances to join in the home meetings. Those who are reluctant to attend a church service may be willing to accompany a believer such as yourself to the non-threatening setting of your home, strictly on the basis of the trust they have in you, via the light of the Christ within you. This makes the small group a great opportunity for evangelism.